BRIDGES TO ISLAM

A CHRISTIAN PERSPECTIVE ON FOLK ISLAM

OTHER BOOKS BY PHIL PARSHALL

The Fortress and the Fire

Muslim Evangelism

Lifting the Veil

Beyond the Mosque

The Cross and the Crescent

Understanding Muslim Teaching and Traditions (formerly titled *Inside the Community*)

The Last Great Frontier

Divine Threads Within a Human Tapestry

BRIDGES TO ISLAM

A CHRISTIAN PERSPECTIVE ON FOLK ISLAM

PHIL PARSHALL

FOREWORD BY J. CHRISTY WILSON, JR.

Authentic

ATLANTA · LONDON · HYDERABAD

Authentic Publishing
We welcome your questions and comments.

USA	PO Box 444, 285 Lynnwood Ave, Tyrone, GA, 30290
	www.authenticbooks.com
UK	9 Holdom Avenue, Bletchley, Milton Keynes, Bucks, MK1 1QR
	www.authenticmedia.co.uk
India	Logos Bhavan, Medchal Road, Jeedimetla Village, Secunderabad
	500 055, A.P.

Bridges to Islam
ISBN-13: 978-1-932805-82-6
ISBN-10: 1-932805-82-6

All Scripture quotations, unless otherwise indicated, are taken from the NEW
AMERICAN STANDARD BIBLE ®, Copyright © 1960, 1962, 1963, 1968, 1971, 1972,
1973, 1975, 1977, 1995 by The Lockman Foundation. Used by permission.

Cover design: Paul Lewis
Interior design: Angela Lewis
Editorial team: Megan Kassebaum, Dana Carrington

Printed in the United States of America

CONTENTS

FOREWORD

The first time I met the author of this book was more than a decade ago, just before the blood bath that resulted in the independence of the country in which Phil Parshall was a resident. Two other speakers and I had been invited to a conference there. With the increasingly tense situation, notices were sent canceling the convention. But with a communications blackout, the word never got through. We arrived at the airport, but no one met us. Taking a taxi, we finally found the right address. When we walked in, Phil and Julie Parshall looked at us as if we had come from outer space. They soon regained their composure and set about to reconstitute the conference. With offices and schools already closed because of the emergency, more people were free to attend, and God blessed the meetings in a singular way. After the conference, we flew out on one of the last planes to leave before hostilities broke out. But the Parshalls and others stayed through it all.

During this experience, I came to discover that Phil Parshall is not simply a theoretical Islamics scholar. He, like Ezekiel of old, has "sat where they sat." He therefore writes from firsthand experience and love for the people he has served for so long.

As Phil Parshall points out in this fascinating study, the majority of the people in the world of Islam are influenced by mysticism. If we are to appreciate the practical outworkings of the Muslim religion, which now claims one-sixth of the human race as adherents, we need to understand folk Islam. This book provides such a bridge. But the author does not stop with merely an intellectual portrayal of Islamic mysticism. He also presents practical ways to acquaint folk Muslims with the God and Father of our Lord Jesus Christ "in whom we live and move and have our being." As he states, "Few folk Muslims have received a relevant explanation of salvation in Christ."

This interesting publication brings out the fact that Islamic mysticism is the reason many Muslims are so open to prayer in the name of Christ. For example, several years ago in Kabul, a friend came to me with a problem. His uncle needed a cataract operation, and my friend had taken him to a government hospital. But the staff members said there would not be a bed available for three months. My friend's uncle could not remain in the capital that long, for he had come from the central highlands and had to get back to his farm. The Muslim friend asked whether I knew the head of the hospital. I told him I did. He then asked me to write a note to him explaining the problem. I said that I did not need to write but would just speak to Him. He asked me what the name of the head of the hospital was. I said, "His name is the Lord Jesus Christ. He is the Head of every hospital." I then prayed with the two men in their language and asked them to go back. A few hours later, my friend returned. He said, "You do know the Head of that hospital! As soon as we got back, they were just discharging a patient and they accepted my uncle in his place and put him in his bed, which was still warm."

This book also demonstrates that folk Muslim leaders or *pirs* are viewed as mediators between man and God and thus have healing powers. This sets the stage for a striking redemptive analogy with the great "mediator between God and men, the man Christ Jesus. . . . Who went about doing good and healing all who were oppressed of the devil." One missionary worked among Muslims for fifteen years and saw few results. On a furlough he attended meetings where people were healed through prayer as is described in James 5:14–15. When he returned to his field, he not only preached the gospel but also prayed for healing in the name of the risen Christ. Through the demonstration of God's restoring power, more Muslims came to Christ in one service than in all the years of his former ministry among them. This is an area in missions that has long been neglected. This book underscores the way healing ministries can be a bridge to reaching Muslims for Christ.

Frequent references in this significant book are quoted from Bishop John A. Subhan, who wrote his testimony under the title *How a Sufi Found His Lord.* When I met this man of God I heard him tell his story in more detail. As a Muslim Sufi he was studying in an Islamic theological school. He had been taught that God caused the likeness of Jesus to fall on Judas, and that Jesus was then taken to heaven and Judas was crucified in his place. But as he read the description of the passion in the New Testament, he came to the words spoken from the cross, "My God, my God, why hast thou forsaken me?" In meditating on this, he thought to himself, "Only a good man could have asked this question. Judas was a bad man, and therefore he would not have asked the reason for his being forsaken." From this he concluded that it really was Jesus who was crucified on the cross for his sins, and he made the great discovery that He was his Lord. May this book result in many other folk Muslims finding their real Lord.

J. Christy Wilson, Jr.
Professor of World Evangelization
Gordon-Conwell Theological Seminary

Acknowledgments

The empirical researcher has an advantage over his counterpart who is limited to pursuing his subject in Western libraries. When one's subject deals with experience and emotion as well as cognitive data, it is necessary to reside where the changes are taking place. It has been a special privilege these past few years to be involved in church planting in Muslim villages. My particular focus has been to share the gospel with folk Muslims. In some senses, I have learned more in this short time about grassroots Islam than I did in my first eighteen years of ministry in the same country. Amazingly, one can be surrounded by certain dynamic situations and still be quite unaware of what is happening. This is particularly true if one seeks to understand Islam from a Western perspective—which is what I sought to do during my early years as a missionary.

A number of *Isais* (followers of Jesus) have greatly influenced me in recent years. First there was a highly educated Muslim Background Believer (MBB) who became an intimate friend. It was his task to constantly goad me to discard my presuppositions about Muslim evangelism. At times, our arguments drifted into the late-night hours. Out of these lively sessions a realization slowly emerged that my friend had insights that would prove invaluable to the future of the evangelization of Muslims, not only locally, but also, to some extent, worldwide. I will forever be grateful to the Lord for this man's persistence.

Decades ago a young Muslim, out of curiosity, purchased a small packet of Christian books from a tall, white-skinned missionary on the crowded streets of a large city. That encounter led to the conversion and spiritual maturity of a flaming evangelist to the Muslim people. It has been my privilege to work as a colleague with this man, as well as to sit at his feet as an inquisitive student.

What a joy to see God work in hearts! The recent MBBs are significant in quality. How amazing to see the intellectual grasp of simple village people who have come to Christ out of a background of folk Islam. The hours spent discussing the Word of God by the light of barn lanterns have been precious. Truly these men have been teachers as well as students.

An extremely well-educated and renowned Muslim has become an intimate friend of mine during these months of researching and preaching. Although our religious differences have been clearly enunciated, still he has been graciously willing to guide me through the intricacies of Islamic mysticism as few could do. This respected devout Muslim opened his heart and home and introduced me to his friends in a manner unknown to me in my years of missionary experience. In a special way, this friend is the dynamic behind this book.

It would be my desire to further identify these men, as well as other people and places mentioned in this book. In the larger interest of Muslim evangelism, I must refrain from doing so. I can, however, give a clear expression of appreciation to my wife, Julie, for her supportive role as a critic, guide, secretary, and dispenser of often-needed encouragement. Our daughter, Lindy, bravely (but not without tears) endured the pangs of separation as she attended a boarding school several thousand miles away from us in order that our ministry during those years could be a reality.

Our mission team, as well as our supporters in the States, continues to be a source of inspiration and motivation to us to continue in the battle. William Wells graciously assisted me in the preparation of the final manuscript of this book. I am indebted to him.

The last word of acknowledgment belongs to my Savior, Jesus Christ. Without His sustaining empowerment, all done would be but wood, hay, and stubble. With Him, I am privileged to minister a message with the permanence of gold, silver, and precious stones.

INTRODUCTION

Why would a genius in the field of physics desire to become a Muslim mystic? Are not the two paths antithetical? Abdus Salam, a Nobel Prize winner, was interviewed for *The Illustrated Weekly of India*:

> We asked him about Sufism, and Professor Salam said he was deeply interested in Sufism, but he could not claim to be a Sufi himself.
>
> A "Sufi," he said, "is someone with direct personal experience. If Allah grants me such an experience, I will be grateful. My father was a Sufi."[1]

Perhaps Salam would agree with Professor William Nilsson, who has said that "there exists in every man a dormant longing to enter into communion with the divine, to feel himself lifted up from the temporal into the spiritual."[2] Certainly Christianity has had its outstanding mystics. Even today there are whole denominations with Christian worship forms that are mystical in origin and expression.

Islam is in tension. On the one hand we find orthodoxy with its rigid code of ritual and laws. The *madrasas* (Muslim religious schools) prepare leaders who are totally committed to a meticulous keeping of the teachings of the Quran and Hadith (traditions). These men are deeply offended by the thought that Islam could be anything other than legalistic. The closest biblical counterparts of these Muslim priests would be the Pharisees with whom Jesus interacted in New Testament times.

1

On the other hand, perhaps 70 percent of all Muslims in the world are influenced by a system we could properly term folk Islam. This book will focus on this major bloc of Muslims that the orthodox community considers aberrant. Bill Musk has aptly summarized the practices of this folk expression of Islam:

> Popular Islam has added a whole life-way of animistic beliefs and practices. The use of the rosary for divining and healing, the use of amulets and talismans, the use of hair-cuttings and nail-trimmings, the belief and practice of saint-worship, the use of charms, knots, magic, sorcery, the exorcism of demons, the practice of tree and stone worship, cursing and blessing—these and many other animistic practices belie the gap between the theological religion and the actual religion.[3]

Perhaps this revelation about animism within Islam will come as a shock to the reader. We have been taught to think of Muslims as homogeneous and Islam as monolithic. The image of Muslims lined up in the mosque for prayer five times a day has been etched deeply into our minds by the media. There has been little understanding of what occurs in the privacy of a Muslim home or within the confines of a *pir's* annual meeting. (A *pir* is a mystically oriented Muslim spiritual guide.) This tension between orthodox and folk Islam is commented on by Erich W. Bethmann.

> Islamic theologians desire to enforce the principles of early Islam without conceding a single point. The slightest aberration means to them a negation of the whole of Islam. They claim, in fact, that the sorry state of the Islamic world is caused by the unfaithfulness of the Muslims to the principles enunciated in the Quran and Hadith.[4]

It was my privilege to spend three weeks touring the island of Mindanao in the southern Philippines. This area is a Muslim stronghold. However, I noted innumerable practices that were typical of folk Islam. The people seemed unaware that their religious rites were outside of those permitted by orthodoxy. This observation is confirmed by Peter G. Gowing, one of the world's leading experts on Filipino Islam.

It is important to stress, however, that identification of non-Islamic features is usually an exercise in which outsiders engage. For the Filipino Muslims their religion is nothing less than Islam. Most of them have little awareness of the synthesis which their beliefs and customs actually represent. Indeed, there have been instances in which foreign Muslim teachers have tried to say that this or that Muslim custom was un-Islamic, only to be repudiated by the local religious leaders on the grounds that *they* [the foreigners] were the ones deficient in Islam. Moreover, virtually everything we have said about the Muslim religious synthesis can be said about the Islamized peoples elsewhere in the Malay world.[5]

The Arabs feel that Allah has appointed them guardians of the purity of Islam. Thus we are finding that they are sending missionaries to Muslims in order to bring the wandering back into the fold. Throughout Mindanao, I met with Egyptian missionaries who were ministering with the financial backing of Saudi Arabia. Also, a number of mosques and *madrasas* had been erected recently in remote areas. These had signs in front that acknowledge the building was a gift of Saudi Arabia or Libya.

A SPIRITUAL VACUUM

Islam, as a theological system, is rigid and unyielding. It not only offers its positive message for obtaining salvation, but also attacks some of the basic tenets of Christianity (e.g., "Christ is not the Son of God"; "Jesus did not die on the cross"; "The Bible has been changed and corrupted in transmission down through the centuries"). However, as millions of Muslims move beyond cold, dead orthodoxy, we see them desiring that felt needs be met. Their hearts cry out for fulfillment in a love relationship to a more personal God. This shift away from firmly established guidelines for faith and practice has created serious anomalies. Yet, we must understand why Muslims all over the world are in quest of a reality beyond cognitive data.

Has a spiritual vacuum developed that can be filled with a warm, vital relationship to God through Jesus Christ? Is the longing for love—both to God and to man—not a primary biblical teaching? What about the fear that grips a Muslim household and causes people to engage in animistic practices to ward off evil spirits? Is Christ not the path to release from fear? Did Jesus not say, "Peace I give unto you"? Many Muslims are totally frustrated in their attempt to gain salvation through an interminable system of laws and rituals. Can grace not point to a better way? Islam gives no assurance of eternal life to its followers. How much better the comfort of 1 John 5:13, which assures us that we can know we have obtained eternal salvation from sin through Christ.

This book will seek to interact with the history, belief, and practices of folk Islam. Sufism will be one of the major focuses of this study, as it is a fairly well-defined influence within folk Islam. Apart from historical notes, I am not emphasizing the philosophical aspects of Sufism. Rather, I am describing Sufism as it is generally practiced among ordinary people. My visits to Sufi meetings have destroyed my long-held presuppositions about the theological and ritual homogeneity of Islam. I will seek to prove my contention that such practices are not the anomalies of a rebel group in an isolated situation. Rather, they are widespread and embrasive.

THE NEED FOR CONCILIATION

It is not my desire to conclude the book at this point. Others have documented Islamic mysticism. The sensitive Christian is motivated to push on and search for a potential bridge between these hungry hearts and the Christ who has promised fulfillment to those who hunger and thirst after righteousness. It is my thesis that, with an appropriate methodology and a firm dependence on the Holy Spirit, we can experience the joy and delight of seeing many questing Muslims come to a vital relationship with the personal God of Scripture who longs to fill empty hearts.

Yes, folk Islam is an erroneous system. Some readers will question how error can ever be utilized as a bridge. One may make the analogy that it is not necessary to agree with all the words and actions of Abraham Lincoln before freely quoting from his profound speeches. Truth is truth wherever it may be found. Folk Islam not only encompasses the spiritually hungry, but also emphasizes doctrinal truths such as monotheism and the unfathomable mercy of God. These teachings have an immense potential to bridge differences as we go to Muslims who have a mystical orientation to religion.

We need to be patient with the seeker who is totally indoctrinated in a system that he has known and experienced since birth. I sometimes become a bit impatient with Christians who believe it is their obligation to share the complete five-minute "gospel package" with as many Muslims as possible. This is often done under the guise of spreading the seed in the shortest time to the most people. The sad fact is that this shotgun approach, either oral or written, can create overwhelming confusion and resistance in the heart of the Muslim. It accomplishes just the opposite of the desired result.

Christianity must be incarnated before the eyes of a Muslim. He must encounter a concerned believer with a deep sensitivity toward him as an individual. The Christian must lay aside his remote-control evangelistic methodology (or frankly term it pre-evangelism). The experience of being born again is instantaneous, but the time and effort that culminate in conversion are great and, at times, tediously frustrating.

These same words are applicable to the newborn Muslim as he takes his first steps as a believer. Unfortunately, extraneous demands have often been laid on the convert in such a way as to create alienation and even reversion to Islam. In this context, I am so glad those who discipled me at the time of my conversion as a teenager did not give up on me because of my cursing, which continued for six months beyond my new birth experience.

A relevant story is narrated in 2 Kings 5. Naaman had received both physical and spiritual healing at the hand of Elisha. In verses 17 and 18, Naaman made two requests of Elisha. One was to take as much soil from Israel as a pair of mules could carry in order that on this sacred ground he could offer burnt offerings and sacrifice to the true God. The other petition was, "When my master enters the temple of Rimmon [a Syrian deity] to bow down and he is leaning on my arm and I bow there also—when I bow down in the temple of Rimmon, may the LORD forgive your servant for this" (v. 18 NIV).

In light of these two requests, one would expect Elisha to commence a forceful lecture on the dangers of syncretism. Amazingly, Elisha simply replied, "Go in peace." It would appear Elisha was counseling patience while his convert made necessary adjustments to his newfound faith.

This is not a plea for pragmatic religious syncretism. I have devoted a significant section in another book, *Muslim Evangelism,* to clarifying this important subject. However, I am convinced that bridges can be built over the abyss that separates Islam and Christianity. This can be done by maintaining a traditional evangelical theology that embraces the inerrancy of Scripture.

A great deal more careful experimentation and involvement is called for. There are few models to guide us in this area. Innovators who will courageously blaze new paths in outreach are desperately needed. Theory needs to be translated to the city of Islamabad and the village of Mohammadpur. Only as Muslims are confronted with a Christian message that is relative and sensitive can we begin to formulate an evaluation that will guide us in the future.

Foundational to mystical Muslims are their poetry and songs, which express their longing for God. Many of these writings are esoteric. Some require interpretation to unlock their meaning. Others are simply beautiful and inspirational. Dhu'l-Nun, an Egyptian, penned these heart-searching lyrics in the very early days of Islamic history:

> I die, and yet not dies in me
> The ardour of my love for Thee,
> Nor hath Thy Love, my only goal,
> Assuaged the fever of my soul.

> To Thee alone my spirit cries;
> In Thee my whole ambition lies.

And still Thy Wealth is far above
The poverty of my small love.

I turn to Thee in my request,
And seek in Thee my final rest;
To Thee my loud lament is brought,
Thou dwellest in my secret thought.[6]

NOTES

1. V. S. Venkatavaradan, "A Genius Called Abdus Salam," *The Illustrated Weekly of India*, February 1–7, 1981, 25.

2. Quoted in Anwarul Karim, *The Bauls of Bangladesh* (Kushtia: Lalon Academy, 1980), 74.

3. Bill Musk, "Popular Islam: Hunger of the Heart," in *The Gospel and Islam: A 1978 Compendium*, ed. Don M. McCurry (Monrovia, Calif.: MARC, 1979), 211.

4. Erich W. Bethmann, *Steps Toward Understanding Islam*, Kohinur series, no. 4 (Washington, D.C.: American Friends of the Middle East, 1966), 62.

5. Peter G. Gowing, *Muslim Filipinos—Heritage and Horizon* (Quezon City: New Day Publishers, 1979), 68–69.

6. Quoted in A. J. Arberry, *Sufism: An Account of the Mystics of Islam* (London: George Allen and Unwin, 1950), 53.

1

MYSTICISM IN HISTORICAL PERSPECTIVE

Every Tuesday and Friday afternoon, in the place beside the church, members desiring to perform the rites kneel before a gigantic white cross on which is nailed perpendicularly the church banner.

As the chorus, consisting mostly of women, wails the hymn of penance, the penitents flog their back with whips spiked with 72 thorns made from twisted "kawad no asero" [steel rope]. Mostly women, the penitents are in blue backless gowns, their long hair stashed beneath scarves. "Patawarin," the chorus cries as thorns pierce supple backs and blood oozes from the wounds. The smell of burning incense and kamangyang fills the plaza.

When a penitent is through, a woman, who acts like an attendant, wipes the wounds with a cloth dipped in vinegar, and salt. These rites can run for three hours.[1]

Could this be a valid description of Christian mysticism? Or considered rites when "healing is either done on the spot or through massage or the laying on of hands, or else certain remedies are prescribed: the drinking of water blessed by the mystic, the rubbing of oil or simple herbal remedies."[2]

Both of these rituals continue today in the Philippines. They are within the general oversight of the Roman Catholic Church, but are neither condemned nor condoned by the church.

On the island of Macao, I visited a Buddhist temple. It was badly in need of repair. In an inner room, I was confronted with a fascinating sight. Around a table sat six monks dressed simply in their yellow robes. The chief priest, a very heavy-set young man in his twenties, sat at the head of the table. He was deeply immersed in meditation and oblivious to all that was going on around him, including the stream of tourists who were staring at him. The other monks kept up a steady chant while occasionally ringing the bells that were in front of them on the table. Dense smoke and nauseating smells from incense filled the air. In such an atmosphere, men were seeking an experience of the divine.

A DEFINITION OF MYSTICISM

It would appear right and proper for the created to long for the creator. A. J. Arberry has defined mysticism as a "constant and unvarying phenomenon of the universal yearning of the human spirit for personal communion with God."[3] Where we find religious expression, there we also find at least a remnant that could be considered mystical. In Christianity, we have Pentecostalism and the charismatic movement. Buddhism has its meditative monks. In India, we observe wandering holy men who by self-denial desire to attain a state of absorption into God.

The Bible is replete with references to mystical experiences. Jacob wrestled with God. David longed for his Lord. Many believe it was Paul who was called up into the third heaven to observe the mysteries of divinity. The apostle John was almost overwhelmed by the visions he received on the isle of Patmos. A study of church history points to mystical saints who have contributed immeasurably to the spread of Christianity. For example, Thomas Aquinas, who wrote in the thirteenth century, was one of the greatest of these who quested for God.

Mystics strive for high levels of purity. They look upon this world as impure. Therefore, they seek to create a sanitized, internalized world that is invulnerable to the crushing realities of life. In this hermetic existence, the mystic is free to contemplate the mysteries of God in peace and serenity. However, it must be pointed out that purity is a concept with varying definitions among the mystics. Some mystics may be sexually promiscuous and use dangerous hallucinogenic drugs. To understand such violations of the standards defining purity, one must understand the subjective nature of mysticism. The lack of allegiance to an authoritative and objective standard or code of life often allows for such behavioral aberrations. The mystic emphasizes the internal and is generally opposed to rigid systems of regulation and ritual. Legalism is regarded as antithetical to "life in the spirit." Kenneth Cragg, the famous Islamist, has stated that mystics "are well known for their relative detachment from canons of orthodoxy and for the way in which they are apt to become, doctrinally, a law unto themselves."[4]

One can understand the conflict that can easily arise between two mystically oriented persons or groups. Both are confident that they know the mind of God and that their channel of information from the Lord is direct and unencumbered. On one occasion, for example, two missionaries were discussing a proposed trip to a village. One of the men was the leader of the mission. He felt strongly that his colleague should join him in the trip. The second missionary was even more convinced that this was not the right thing to do. Both godly men ended up in the embarrassing position of defending their conflicting positions by appealing to the mystical assurance that God was on their side of the argument. Taken to extremes, mysticism can truly lead to each person becoming a law unto himself.

> It is usually maintained in mystical literature that God, inaccessible as He may be to ordinary believers and to ordinary human faculties, is nonetheless supremely accessible to the mystic. The mystic, if anyone does, achieves cognitive, affective, unitive, relation with God.[5]

A DESCRIPTION OF SUFISM

From this point through chapter 2, I will focus on Sufism, for without understanding Sufism, one cannot understand folk Islam.

The nickname *Sufi* is derived from the Arabic word that means "wool." (Other attempts at linguistic analysis of the word *Sufi* are inconclusive.) The word appears to have been applied initially to Abu Hashim Uthman ben Sharik of Kufa, who died in 776. By the middle of the ninth century, the term was widely applied to holy men who practiced austerity.[6] The generally accepted view, then, is that the nickname refers to the mystics' teaching about austerity and their simple style of dress.

Sufism is the embrasive influence of mysticism within Islam. I particularly like to use the word *influence* in attempting to define and understand Sufism. Mystical Muslims may or may not fit into categories or orders. Their behavior and even doctrine may differ widely among themselves, yet there are definite patterns within their fraternity that have the effect of creating homogeneity within heterogeneity. A Muslim has defined Sufism as "truth without form."[7] That may be basically correct, but the so-called truth will be identifiable as we study the way it is expressed within the multiple sects found throughout the Islamic world.

John A. Subhan, himself an Indian Sufi convert to Christianity, has declared that Sufism, like other forms of mysticism, emphasizes not the performances of external ritual, but rather the activities of the inner self.[8]

> It will suffice here to say that Sufism or Muslim mysticism owes its origin, in the main, to a feeling of dissatisfaction with teaching that offers a purely transcendent God, and to a break away from the hard legalism of Islam. The Sufi seeks a direct approach to the Divine Being and indeed claims to have immediate experience of Him. Through the centuries there has thus been developed a religion of the heart and men have become "drunk" with the love of God. Poetry has been wedded to passion in worship at this shrine.[9]

The Muslim mystic hopes, even in this mortal life, to win a glimpse of immortality. This is done by passing away from self into an absorption in the consciousness of God. He feels confident this experience will lead him, after death, to enjoy an eternity with his Lord and with the angels and prophets. The Sufi generally places more emphasis on his relationship to God in this life than on that which is to come.

Reynold A. Nicholson has succinctly stated the Sufi view of the law:

> The ecstatic state knows no law, and therefore "the man of God is beyond infidelity and religion." But except by Sufis of the baser sort, this is not understood as sanctioning irreligious and immoral behavior. The true saint keeps the law, not because he is obliged to do so, but through being himself one with God.[10]

Al-Ghazzali, the most famous of all Sufis, spoke of worship as a "form that the law made[,] and devotion is given reality by acquiring it. Its spirit and inner life are humbleness, intention, presence of the heart, and singleness of devotion."[11] I will be referring to this prolific writer throughout this book. Of all writers, Al-Ghazzali has best captured the essence of Sufism.

Another writer has a profound insight when he says that Sufism "stresses the individual rather than society, the eternal rather than the historical, God's love rather than His power, and the state of man's heart rather than behavior."[12] One Muslim author has taken exception to the idea that the mystic has any real concern for the future life.

> A true Muslim, in the Sufi sense of the term, does not care at all for heaven or hell. Neither the temptation of heaven, its cool gardens, its virgins and beautiful lads and divine meat and drink nor the fears of hell-fire can produce any appreciable effect in his love-intoxicated heart. What he cares for, is love. He carefully watches its gradual development, zealously guards it and solemnly follows its dictates. Union with his Beloved is the mission of his life, and to fulfill that

unique mission, he cares for nothing—neither the pleasures and pains of this world, nor those of the next[13]

Asceticism has been dominant among many Muslim mystics. Their doctrine of leaving the world spiritually has often led to renouncing material possessions. Many of the early Sufi missionaries endured great hardships as they crossed formidable geographical boundaries in order to share with others their unique view of "enlightenment."

Asceticism for its own sake can cause the adherent to have a rather joyless, negative outlook on the universe. But when self-denial is warmed by spiritual emotion, it creates an attitude of rejoicing in hardship and tribulation.[14] In summary, the words of another Muslim author are shared for the reader's consideration.

> The Sufis are bound by no religious dogma, however tenuous, and use no regular place of worship. They have no sacred city, no monastic organization, no religious instruments. They even dislike being given any inclusive name which might force them into doctrinal conformity. "Sufi" is no more than a nickname, like "Quaker" which they accept good-humoredly.[15]

A CHRONOLOGICAL OVERVIEW OF SUFI MYSTICISM

Anwarul Karim, an outstanding Bangladeshi scholar, has described the early period of Sufism:

> The first period extended from 661 A.D. to 850 A.D. The Sufi system was on a personal and individual basis. Fear of God, fear of hell, and fear of death, together with a dissatisfaction of the existing system forced these mystics out of their homes and into seclusion. The second period was chiefly developed in Persia during the ninth century. Fear was replaced by divine love. These mystics, who were mostly concerned with metaphysics, had a burning love for the Divine Being which was all absorbing and self-effacing. God was no longer the

great task master, but the soul of beauty and tenderness. This period gave rise to a number of philosophers.[16]

Subhan has noted that there was a progression from asceticism and seclusion to contemplation. From there it was a natural movement to dreaming dreams, seeing visions, and experiencing ecstasy in worship.[17]

Early Muslim asceticism, with its fearful visions of the wrath to come, its fasters and "weepers," its austerities, devotions, and endless litanies, was a forcing-house for mysticism. Since "there is no god but Allah," and to worship Him for the sake of being saved from Hell or rewarded with paradise is to associate with Him a "god," i.e., another object of hope or fear, the ascetic is impelled to trust in Him alone and acquiesce entirely in His will. But these words cannot be the last. Perfect detachment from "gods" involves perfect attachment to God: in mystical language, union with God through *love*. This is the doctrine that inspires all religious and ethical Sufism.[18]

The oldest surviving general account of Sufism, dated 988, is the *Kitab al-luma* of Abu Nasr al-Sarraj. This volume is a series of theological treatises that describe and analyze the doctrines and practices of the Sufis. The author gives particular attention to the technical vocabulary of the movement. One section is devoted to the "imitation of the Prophet," while another seeks to document the saintliness of the Prophet's companions. The writer also discusses miracles and ecstatic utterances. Interestingly, the book concludes with a long and detailed exposure of errors committed by Sufis. The *Kitab al-luma* is very well documented. It abounds in quotations from mystical writers and poets.[19]

It could be said that Arabian mysticism was the outcome of the true devotional spirit of Islam. The roots were the Quran and the Hadith. If mysticism had remained at this level of orthodoxy, it is doubtful that the schisms within Islam would have occurred.[20]

Early orthodox mysticism was based largely on fear. There was an exaggerated consciousness of sin and a great fear of divine retribution.

Out of this fear mystics felt compelled to submit unreservedly to His will. This bondage set the stage for the reform movement that stressed freedom and liberty based on love and intimacy with God. So we find, around the ninth century, a spontaneous break with established rituals. Muslims began experimenting with meditation, which they felt would be the bridge for them to really come to know the God they so systematically yet so lifelessly professed. "In the eighth century Hazrath Rabiya was one of the first to bring the idea of love into Sufism. It was all-absorbing and self-effacing. For Rabiya it was a burning love which scorned to think of Paradise or Hell."[21]

During the ninth century, Christian mysticism made a strong impression on Sufism. Ascetic and quietistic trends of early Sufism were bound to be influenced by the mystical doctrines found among Christians in North Africa and Syria. Many gospel texts and apocryphal sayings of Jesus came to be cited in Sufi hagiologies. Wandering Muslim ascetics came into contact with Christian mystics. And the theory of gnosis as it developed in Sufism suggests that Muslim ascetics were influenced by Gnostics.[22]

In this historical summary, it is important to note the conversion to mysticism of one of the great Sufis of all times. It was in the eleventh century that Al-Ghazzali lived and distinguished himself as one of the most noted academicians of his day. As a professor at the University of Baghdad, Al-Ghazzali came to feel totally unworthy before God. More than anything else, he desired to avoid hell and attain assurance of eternal life. At age thirty-seven, after a severe inner struggle, he left Baghdad to take up the life of a wandering ascetic. This crisis experience of conversion was to have a profound effect on the future course of mysticism. Al-Ghazzali became a peerless writer on Sufism. His influence continues unabated.

By the middle of the eleventh century there were no fewer than twelve sects of Sufism. Ten were considered "orthodox" and two were "heretical." These sects were named after their reputed founders. A distinctive body of doctrine formed within each group.

In the thirteenth century the classic period of Sufism commenced. This new epoch was marked by the advent of three famous mystical poets of Persia: Faridud-Din Attar, Jalalud-Din Rumi, and Shaykh Sadi. The writings of these poets have greatly influenced the religious thought of Muslims in the East. They continue to be widely disseminated and studied by Muslims throughout the world.

By the thirteenth century, Sufism was ready to be launched as a missionary movement. It had an ethos, however nebulous. It had a focus on felt needs. Muslims were prepared for a revivalist message that would allow them to remain Muslims and yet experience a new, fresh, and meaningful personal encounter with God. Muslim armies were marching eastward. Accompanying them were Sufi soldiers, priests, and businessmen. They would make an irreversible impact on the non-Muslim world.

One of the most positive features of Sufism in this time of expansion was its ability to merge into the cultural and religious stream of the people. Southeast Asia was ripe for Sufi-type missionary activity. Peter G. Gowing and William Henry Scott have pointed out that "the end products of the particular acculturative situation of two contacting groups are: the time factor; the demographic situation; ecology; and the characteristics of the people involved."[23] History indicates that these factors converged to the benefit of Sufi expansionist goals.

Syncretism was not offensive to Sufi missionaries. Gowing and Scott explain the methodology:

> Are the "foreign" agents of religious acculturation insistent about the features of their own religion? Do they permit the indigenous population to combine some of their native religious beliefs with the new religious beliefs being introduced? This is a very crucial factor affecting what happens to the product: if sufficient force is used to keep the new religion "pure," the indigenous population may not accept any of it, because it is not offered in a permissive atmosphere.[24]

There is no better case study of Sufi expansion than events in the Indian subcontinent, for Hinduism is exceptionally syncretistic. Hindus always stand ready to accept a "new path" as long as it doesn't make exclusive claims. Sufism was able to assimilate many Indian cultural and religious rituals. A significant number of Hindus felt comfortable as they shifted allegiance to a religion that looked and felt familiar. True, many Hindus converted under duress. But very soon they came to regard Islam as their own. It is also true that not all Islamic teaching was influenced by Sufis. Some propagation was more orthodox in doctrine and ritual. But overall one finds extensive marks of Sufism throughout the subcontinent.

India, Pakistan, and Bangladesh together have a Muslim population of around 375 million. This is about one-third of the world's Islamic population. These three countries, it must be understood, geographically and demographically constituted one entity prior to 1947. This must be kept in mind when the words *India* or *subcontinent* are used in a historical sense.

> Sufism, with its warm, mystical yearning after union and fellowship with God, nowhere found a more suitable soil in which to thrive than India, where the very atmosphere was charged with a deep religious longing to find God with the result that today it is estimated that fully two-thirds of India's Muslim population are under the influence of some one or other of the *darwish* orders.[25]

After the military conquest of northern India, Sufis began to pour into the country. This peaceful and tolerant element of Islam impressed the conquered Hindus, whereas the more fanatical and militaristic orthodox Muslim priests were feared and hated. Almost all willing conversions were the result of the preaching of Sufi missionaries.

Islam did not conquer nor convert all of India's Hindus. Many resisted the imposition of a foreign religion that they considered antithetical to that which had been followed for hundreds of years. However, the syncretistic tendencies of Hinduism helped smooth the path toward coexistence. This communal harmony disintegrated at the time of the forced creation of Pakistan in 1947. The unwise geographical division of the land that became East and West Pakistan led to another convulsive civil war in 1971 that resulted in the creation of Bangladesh.

Islam seemed unable to infuse the same strength into Indian Muslims as it did into the Arabs. Climatic conditions and the vastness of the country, as well as the natural philosophic bent of the Indian mind, were the chief factors that stood in the way of true, all-embrasive Islamic influence on India. Yet Sufism made very significant gains on the subcontinent in the twelfth, thirteenth, and fourteenth centuries. In the history of Indian thought, the fifteenth and sixteenth centuries may be characterized as the time when two different sets of ideas and separate systems of thought—Indian as well as Islamic—were fused into one.[26]

A Muslim author writing of early Sufi missionary efforts in India explains the approach:

> Among the preachers of Islam in India the Sufi, whose training was more ascetic, was closer to the masses of the people than the theologian who was generally a fanatic and lacked character and spiritual sensitiveness. In city, town, and village the Sufi formed himself into a pivot of an inner circle of non-Muslims, mainly low-caste Hindus, whom he attracted by his spirituality and humanity. The outer circle was gradually sucked into Islam by an indirect rather than a direct appeal which began with the non-Muslim's admiration for the individual Sufi, and continued through his observation of Muslim egalitarianism in the inner circle.[27]

Another writer highlights "indomitable zeal, uncommon piety, and widely believed miracles" as the authentication of early Sufi ministry.[28] These mystics led very simple and pious lives. They shunned worldly comforts and pleasures. They served God with single-minded devotion. Their spiritual policy was peace with all. Military methods of inducing conversion to Islam were abhorrent to the Sufi messengers of love and peace. They preached toleration and conciliation toward all men of all races and religions. Karim comments on the syncretistic tendency of early Sufi missionaries when he states that "Sufis looked upon all religions as different roads leading to the same destination. . . . These mystics believed that the Hindus could attain spiritual greatness to the same degree as Muslims."[29]

Lajwanti Rama Krishna has well described the movement of Sufism away from its Islamic roots into a state where many Sufis (though not all, by any means) would not be considered Muslims in the strict sense of the word.

> The Sufis who came to India with the object of leading the Indians to the Beloved by Muhammad's path, did credible work for some years. Then the old Indian vigor asserted itself and in its turn influenced the Sufi beliefs. The mystics therefore absorbed the best of Islam and Hinduism and developed a new sort of Sufi thought, more Indian than foreign in character. Anxious to carry this new thought to the masses, they versified it in their language. In [troublesome] times, the Sufis maintained with their preachings the mental balance of the different communities and, through their poems, sent the message of peace, unity, and love to almost every home and hamlet.[30]

I once visited in a home in the Indian subcontinent where I was introduced to a young man with long, flowing hair. Within a few minutes, it was obvious I was interacting with an extremely intelligent person. He was from a Muslim home, but identified himself as a Sufi as well as a follower of Krishna. At one point, he stated that I could choose a tree of any size and after he applied a certain mixture to it, the tree would definitely die within three days. If it didn't, I could feel free to shoot him! This Sufi seemed to be possessed of very definite mystical power—at least in speech, if not in deed. I came away from our encounter feeling that Sufism is indeed alive and well in the subcontinent.

But Islamic mysticism is by no means geographically bound. During a trip to North Africa early in 1982, I was able to visit the *mazar* (the shrine of a famous Muslim mystic) of Sidi Abderrahmane. It is located in the famous Casbah area of the city of Algiers. This *mazar* is the second oldest monument in Algeria. Abderrahmane died in 1471 and is known today as the "protector of Algiers." People come from great distances to visit this shrine. Most of the devotees are women.

Inside the small room I noted ostrich eggshells; banners and chandeliers hanging from the ceiling; lanterns and mirrors placed around the large tomb, which was covered with embroidered cloth; and a picture of the hand of Fatima with an eye in the middle of the palm. Offerings of bread, cloth, candles, and money were presented in memory of Abderrahmane. There was a place to pray toward Mecca in one corner of the room.

There are many other illustrations of animism on the folk level among Muslims in North Africa.

> Certain superstitious practices in North African Islam have been traced by sociologists to Berber origins; curiously enough identical forms of animism and superstition made their appearance in India and have been attributed to Hindu influences. The two streams are largely unconnected, and have their common origin, perhaps, in the very nature of mass belief.[31]

S. Q. Fatemi explains the Sufi influence in Malaysia: "The reason why these Sufis were so successful in spreading Islam among the Malays was the eclecticism and the elasticity of Sufism, which had made it adaptable and therefore acceptable to the Malay masses."[32] Another author has pointed out that in Malaysia "Islam was spread by Sufi missionaries and to such men were attributed supernatural or 'magical' powers."[33]

Sufi syncretism evidently was instrumental in the southern island of Mindanao in the Philippines becoming Islamized.

> The rapid Islamization of the Filipino Maranao was due to Sufi missionaries who identified themselves closely with the people they converted, and the fact that the faith was easy to learn, and focused on the belief in one supreme God—Allah. As former President Antonio Isidro of the Mindanao State University pointed out: "The rituals are easy to perform, and the people are not forced to give up many of their pre-

Islamic customs and practices—retaining much of the old
traditions."[34]

During my tour of the southern Philippines, I noted a number of
evidences of folk Islam. In Zamboanga, I visited in the home of a "jinn
man." His eight-foot-by-eight-foot slatted bamboo house was built on
stilts twelve feet above the ocean. (Some thirty thousand Muslims are
packed into a few acres of such homes.) His house was identifiable by
a white cloth tied on a bamboo pole high above his dwelling. This aged
and feeble Muslim priest graciously talked to our small party for thirty
minutes. He showed us the special clothes he wears when he ministers.
Healing is an important part of his activities. He lays his hands on the
area of complaint in a sick person's body and prays in the name of Allah
for healing and restoration. Sacrifice of animals, in God's name, is also
a part of his ministry.

David W. Shenk, an expert on African Islam, comments on Sufism
as he observed it in his travels.

> In Muslim communities across the African Continent saint
> veneration and mysticism abound. Recently I visited central
> Java, Bangladesh, and southern Yugoslavia, and found
> that in these widely diverse Muslim communities, saint
> veneration and mysticism are persistent. And the experience
> and practice of saint veneration were amazingly consistent.
> This is especially remarkable, because in each community
> the orthodox institutions are always in tension with these
> widespread popular expressions of Islam.[35]

Sufism, then, is a historical phenomenon as well as a contemporary
happening. There is probably no country in the world where its direct
influence is not felt.

SUFI ORDERS

It has been calculated that 70 percent of all Muslims are acquainted
with the Sufi orders within Islam. Millions have chosen to follow one or
another path. The *pir* of their order has become a very special guide to

them, not only in matters of the spirit, but also in all worldly matters. The origin of Sufi orders has been described in these words:

> Sufi theosophy had in its origin a great tendency to individualism. In its inception it was neither meant for the ordinary common folk, nor for any coterie of intellectuals. Illumination of the individual soul by the culture of one's own self was the aim and object of the early Sufis. Great Sufis of the eighth and ninth centuries A.D. achieved this illumination by individual exertion, mortification, and austerity. This individualistic tendency among Sufis led each individual to the way of thinking out a theosophic system according to his own mentality and intellectual attainments. Hence, each system of Sufi theosophy bears a clear stamp of an individual who shaped it and worked it out in the line invented or discovered by him. In this way, when one system took final shape and when following that definite system, any individual attained the ideal as desired by him, others with similar tendencies accepted the path laid down by him. This was a kind of servile imitation; yet it was helpful to many. In any case, the disciples clung round the master and formed a group to be named after the master or founder. As it is a case with all groups or sects, after the formation of a well-defined order, many new formalities and rituals were, in course of time, introduced. The beginning of Sufi orders is thus as old as the origin of Sufism itself.[36]

Sufis may differ in name, customs, dress, meditations, recitations, and even doctrines, yet they have in common their quest for God. It is not possible here to describe all of their various orders. In fact, it is not possible even to document how many sects there are within Islam. Also, to add to the confusion is the reality of hundreds, if not thousands, of subsects within each major order. These smaller groups gather around a *pir* who may be expounding teaching quite divergent from that of the order he professes to follow. Yet it is essential to attain some measure of understanding about these orders. I shall touch briefly on the four major sects of Sufism found in the Indian subcontinent today. Literally millions of Muslims are attached to these orders. Much can be learned about folk Islam from a careful study of these groups. It will be noted that distinctions among the orders are not doctrinal; rather the uniqueness of each group often centers around personalities.

CHISHTI ORDER

The Chishti order was the first important Sufi sect to be established in India. It was founded by Khwaja Abu Ishaq Shami Chishti. He migrated from Asia Minor and settled at Chisht in Khurasan and consequently was called Chishti.

The most famous saint of this order was Khwaja Muinud-Din, the sponsor of the Chishti movement in India. He was born in the town of Sanjar in Sistan in 1142. His ancestors for several generations were reputed to be mystics. On one occasion a holy man met Muinud-Din and was said to have transmitted spiritual power to him by taking a piece of bread, chewing it, and then giving it to Muinud-Din to eat. This bread, having been in close contact with the holy man, was believed to have possessed supernatural power that was imparted to Muinud-Din. This incident illustrates common Sufi teaching that spiritual vitality can be transmitted through a material substance that has been in intimate contact with the person of a holy man.

Muinud-Din traveled extensively to visit the shrines of departed saints. There he would meditate and seek to attain some of their spiritual power. He eventually settled in Ajmir, India, where he died at the age of eighty-nine. His resting place has become the Mecca of the adherents of the Chishti order. On the anniversary of his death, Muslims from all over the world make a pilgrimage to his tomb.

Toward the close of the twelfth century, there arose a great controversy among Muslims regarding the use of music among Chishtis. Orthodox Muslim leaders were extremely displeased with the Sufi practice of singing the praises of Allah. Such music was considered to be forbidden by the Quran and Hadith. One of the Chishti saints described music as "the hearing of harmonious sounds which move the heart, and kindle the fire of love for God."[37] Chishtis always have had a heart for music. Singing and playing instruments are central in their expression of hunger for God.

Babu Farid was a popular Indian Chishti who died in 1265. There are many stories regarding his austerity and self-mortification. At one period in his life he prayed all night while suspended by his feet in a well. He persisted in this practice for forty nights. The ritual was a closely guarded secret while it was being performed. Because of his ability to perform miracles, Babu Farid had 101 titles bestowed upon him. A few of these titles are the Present, the Praised, the Perfect, the Truthful, the Patient, the Majestic, the Inward, the Outward, the Light of God, the Grace of God, the Liberality of God, and the Spirit of God. These titles are often repeated as a charm to heal the sick.

Babu Farid is buried in a tomb in the Punjab of Pakistan. His mausoleum contains a door called the Door of Paradise, which is opened only on the anniversary of his death. All devotees make a point of passing through the door on this auspicious occasion. It is said that Nizamud-Din was present at the shrine when he had a vision of Muhammad standing at the door and saying, "Whosoever shall enter this door shall be saved." Since that time, this entrance has been known as the Door of Paradise.

The Chishti order is the most colorful of the Sufi sects. Its practices are among those most vehemently denounced by the orthodox Muslim. Yet they continue in fervor throughout the subcontinent.

SUHRAWARDI ORDER

Shihabud-Din Suhrawardi of Baghdad was the founder of this order of Muslim mystics. The man who did most to spread the influence of this sect in India was Bahaud-Din Zakariya, who was born in Multan, Pakistan, in 1182. Early in his life he made a pilgrimage to Mecca and from there proceeded to Baghdad where he became a student of Shihabud-Din Suhrawardi. Soon he attained "perfection," was appointed head of state by his master, and was sent back to India.

Stories abound about Bahaud-Din and his unusual experiences. He is said to have been the recipient of three mantles, symbols that served to indicate that he held the highest authority in the order. He dreamed that he received one of these mantles from God. Upon awakening, he found that the mantle was on his body.

At one point, Bahaud-Din had an ecstatic experience in which he heard a voice from heaven conferring on him two names: the Great and the Enlightener. Soon thereafter he declared,

> Any needy person who recites the following invocation, which contains all the titles which I have received from God; will have all his needs supplied, and God will forgive his sins and increase the light of his faith; and if a person recites this prayer every day of his life, I promise to stand as surety for him in order to obtain for him the rewards of paradise in the day of judgment.[38]

The invocation was an exaltation of Bahaud-Din that concluded with a petition for him to fulfill the desires of the supplicant. This mystic died in 1267 in Multan, where thousands of Muslim devotees now visit his tomb.

Shaykh Ahmad Mashuq was another prominent saint of this order. Prior to conversion he was a merchant with a reputation as a drunkard. Once, while bathing in a river, he prayed, "O God, I will not go up out of the water, till Thou hast revealed to me the dignity that I have in Thy sight." In reply, he heard a voice saying to him, "So great is thy dignity in my sight that on the day of judgment a large number of sinners will receive pardon through thy intercession." He prayed again, "O Lord, this is not enough—further increase my dignity out of Thy bounteous mercy." Then the voice replied, "I am thy lover and thou art my Beloved: go now and make others my seekers." From that time he came to be known by the title the Beloved.[39] Such is the type of mystical experience that launched Muslim saints into their exalted positions of spiritual leadership.

Yet another saint, Hafiz Muhammad Ismail, was born in 1586. When he was twelve years old he was given the task of grinding corn. The story is told of how his master paid him a surprise visit and was astonished to see the young boy deeply engaged in meditation. Meanwhile the handmill was grinding the corn automatically.

Ismail was told later to milk a large number of cows. It was noted that the cows he milked yielded unusually large quantities of milk. Soon all the neighbors brought their cows to Ismail to be milked. Within a short time he was recognized as a saint. He traveled to Lahore, where he started a school for the purpose of instructing pupils in the art of reading the Quran. It is believed that he possessed such power as a teacher that each of his students memorized the Quran in a miraculously short time. He is reported to have declared that this virtue would continue to be potent at his grave after his death. Many young people went to his *mazar* for the purpose of memorizing the Quran. It was also believed that, by eating the herbs and leaves of plants that grew close to the tomb, the intellect was quickened so that the Quran was more easily committed to memory.

Shah Dawla was sold into slavery to a Hindu family at a young age following the death of his widowed mother. At his master's house he exhibited great piety and was faithful in discharging all of his responsibilities. Soon he was set free in recognition of his holiness. Shah Dawla was initiated into sainthood by the great *pir,* Sayyid Nasir Mast.

There are many tales of miracles associated with Shah Dawla's life and ministry. Chief among these are the births of "rat children." These children, born through his intercessory power, had minute heads, large ears, and rat-like faces, and were without understanding or power of speech. Although they were repulsive, no contempt of them was to be shown. If anyone violated this prohibition, his next child would be born in a similar state.

Musa Shahi Suhag founded a new sect of the Suhrawardi order that is named after him. He dressed like a woman and lived among eunuchs who were dancers by profession. In his native city of Ahmedabad there was once a great scarcity of rain. The people prevailed upon Shah Musa to pray to Allah for relief. His prayer was, "O my husband, if you are not going to send rain at once, I am going to deprive myself of these bridal ornaments." He was about to break his bangles when clouds appeared on the horizon. Soon it began to rain heavily and continued to do so for several days. Upon his death in 1449, his disciples appointed a successor whom they adorned like his master in the dress and ornaments of a bride.

Such are some of the practices of leading saints within the Suhrawardi order of Sufis.

QADIRI ORDER

This order was established in India three hundred years after the death of its founder, Shaykh Abdul-Qadir Julani (also spelled Gilani). The key propagator was Muhammad Ghawth, tenth in line of succession to Julani. The son of Ghawth, Abdul Qadir II, was an ascetic saint who shunned all worldly honors. Once, when a prince invited Abdul Qadir II to the palace, he declined to go and instead sent this stanza.

> I have no door to which to go
> From this one door of Allah.
> While seated here, come weal or woe,
> I am content with either.
> Whoso, in this world, wears the cloak
> Provided by the King of Love,
> Feels a delight he could not have
> Though robed in light in heaven above.[40]

Sayyid Bahawal Shah was a saint of this order who used to sit by a riverbank and pass his days in meditation. However, the women of the neighborhood complained to their husbands that when they came to the river they were exposed to the gaze of the *faqir* (a religious person who solicits alms in the name of Islam). Driven away from this place, he settled somewhat further down the bank, where he met with the same complaint. Becoming angry, he smote the river and ordered it to change its course. Immediately the river began to flow at a distance four miles from its original course. Eventually, three wooden pegs were driven in the ground near the saint. Each of these immediately sprouted into a tree.

Two of them are said to still be green. The attendant at his shrine, for a small offering, will give the visitor a bit of the wood from one of these trees. Generally this is made into beads for a rosary.

During his latter days, Bahawal Shah is said to have ridden on a lion and carried a snake in his hand in place of a whip. A shrine was placed over his grave in Lahore.

Haji Muhammad was reported to have received sainthood at the time of his birth. As he grew older, he always had a reputation for hospitality. If his own resources failed, he would beg from door to door until he had collected sufficient food to feed his guests. One day he went to beg for some flour at a neighbor's house. The woman of the house was in the act of kneading dough, but upon seeing the saint at a distance, she hid it quickly under her thigh. She apologized to him for her inability to give him the requested flour. When the saint had departed, the woman realized, to her horror, that the dough had stuck to her body and no amount of effort could release it until her husband went to the saint and, confessing her fault, requested him to pray on her behalf.

Another story illustrates the conflict between mystical saints and orthodox Islam. Muhammad Fudayl, a native of Kabul, went to India and acquired perfection in the mystical path. Upon his return to Kabul, he, being inclined to ecstatic experiences, neglected the obligatory prayers as prescribed by the Quran and Hadith. The *ulama* of Kabul, a community of scholarly leaders, went to him and threatened to punish him if he would not say his prayers. Fudayl argued that prayer could not be performed without the customary ablution, which he said was impossible for him to perform. The ulama, desiring to test the truth of this assertion, brought some water and poured it on Fudayl's arms in an effort to fulfill the requirements of ablution. To the great surprise of all in attendance, the arms and hands of the saint did not even become wet.

The *faqirs* of Naushali, a splinter group of the Qadiri order, hold musical festivals that end in an orgy of emotion. Then these *faqirs* hang upside down on trees, sway violently backward and forward, and shout "illa llah" until they faint from exhaustion.

A rather common belief is illustrated by yet another story. Miyan Mir was a saint whose favorite disciple was Miyan Nattha. Both men lived in a two-story house, Mir living in the upper story and Nattha in the lower. Each night it was Nattha's custom to carry water to his master so he could perform ablutions before prayer. One night Nattha was late in bringing the water. On reaching the room he failed, in spite of a thorough search, to find his master. Being very anxious about his master's sudden disappearance, Nattha spent the whole night seated outside the saint's door awaiting his return. Great was his surprise when, early in the morning, he heard his master shouting from within the room for water to be brought inside. Nattha, curious to know where his master had been during the night and how he had managed to get inside the room, naturally asked for an explanation. The saint, when pressed, replied, "I generally spend my night on Mount Hira, in the vicinity of Mecca, where Prophet Muhammad used to meditate in his early life." It is a common belief that Sufi saints can be spiritually transported to distant places.

NAQSHBANDI ORDER

Khwaja Bahaud-Din Naqshband was the founder of this order. Ahmad Faruqi established the sect in India. The influence of this order was widespread and even affected political conditions in India, Turkey, and Mesopotamia.

A number of miracles were said to have occurred at the birth of Ahmad Faruqi. All the dead saints appeared to his mother and congratulated her on his birth. His father saw Muhammad, in the company of all the prophets, come near the infant and repeat the name of Allah in his ears and enumerate his virtues. Further, we are told that for a whole week from the day of his birth, no musician could play an instrument. Many of them took this to be a sign of God's disapproval of their profession and thus relinquished it. It was said that Ahmad, like Muhammad, was born circumcised.

In 1603, Baqi Billah eulogized Ahmad by saying, "Ahmad has guided us to the true interpretation of Sufi pantheism. In the knowledge of mysticism he is like a sun while we are like planets revolving round him. Indeed, after Muhammad there has never been a saint in dignity equal to him."[41]

Ahmad for a period of time was regarded as an enemy of the state and was imprisoned by the ruler, Jahangir. But within three years Ahmad was able to persuade his enemies of his saintly character. Upon release, he converted Jahangir into his disciple. The emperor, following the advice of his *pir*, proceeded to make several changes in matters of the state. The custom of falling prostrate before the king, which had been in force from the time of Akbar, was discontinued. The use of beef, which had been prohibited, was made permissible. The most important change was that the Islamic code (shariat) was adopted as the law of the state.

Ahmad looked upon himself as a reformer. He regarded it as his duty to purge Sufism of many of the extraneous elements that had become attached to it through its long history. Prohibited were the use of music; dancing while in the state of ecstasy; prostration before one's *pir;* the worship of the saints and shrines; and illuminating the tombs of saints. He also made an effort to harmonize the doctrines of mysticism with the teachings of the Quran and Sunnah (the record of sayings and activities of Muhammad).

Ahmad is credited with performing more than seven hundred miracles. He also is said to have written 644 treatises on various religious subjects. His teachings are mainly embodied in a series of letters that were collected in his lifetime and are now published in three large volumes.

Ahmad was the first of the saints within Islam who claimed for himself and for his three immediate successors the title *Qayyum.* The *Qayyum* is the dignitary on whom the whole order of existence depends, and under whose control are all names, attributes, and things actual and potential. It is through his command that the heavens move in their courses, the waves rise and fall in seas and oceans, the rains fall from heaven, fruits ripen, and day succeeds night. The earth remains motionless or quakes in accordance with his will, and all of its inhabitants receive joy or sorrow, pleasure or pain according to his discretion.

The *Qayyum* is the substance of all that exists. He is the Vicar of God on earth. The Absolute bestows upon him a special essence called *mawhub,* on which depends the subsistence of the universe. This special office was strictly limited to Ahmad and his three successors.

A story is told of how one night after his prayer Ahmad's whole body became so luminous that it dazzled the eyes, and at that moment he received this "revelation" from God: "O, Ahmad! this thy body is made of the residue of the substance of Muhammad's body, which I had reserved for thy sake, for thou wast to be my beloved."

Ahmad claimed he was the custodian of "His Treasury of Mercy." He stated that an infinite number of angels were standing before him with folded hands ready to obey his every command. He further asserted that he had given his son, Said, the seal of the permit to enter heaven on the day of judgment. He declared that all who receive from God a permit to enter heaven must first obtain the permission of his son. Other acts of mercy (such as rescuing sinners from hell and assisting people at the bridge of death) were entrusted to another son and successor, Masum.

The last of the *Qayyums* died in 1739, a time when the Muslim empire was crumbling. By this date the Naqshbandi order had spread to every part of the Muslim world.

In one Muslim country, I was able to visit a reputed *pir* of the Naqshbandi order. After driving seven hours, my friends and I turned off the main road onto a dirt path that led through the fields. We followed fifteen buses as we inched our way along the last six miles of our journey. The buses were filled with boisterous Muslims who were all wearing their prayer hats. The night air was filled with the sound of the chanting of the name of Allah blaring forth from loudspeakers mounted on the buses. The vehicles were stopped several times by local villagers who were collecting donations for the building of new mosques.

As we rounded the last curve we were overwhelmed by what we saw. There in the most remote of villages was what looked like a small town. Hundreds of lights were strung over two mammoth buildings, each the size of a football field. Huge tents had been erected; under these, one hundred thousand devotees were sitting and listening to a fiery orator holding forth regarding the virtues of the *pir*. Scores of small stores were selling everything from tea to religious charms. The government had made special arrangements to bring electricity and even a telephone exchange to the *pir's* home. I was told a runway was soon to be constructed to enable people to fly in to see the *pir*. The two buildings housed religious schools to accommodate students from the first grade through graduate courses.

We were taken to the eating area for a special meal of rice and meat. As we walked around in bare feet (no shoes were allowed on such holy ground) we were amazed to see the enormity of the *pir's* following. We heard the *pir* extolled as a "flower descended from heaven." The meeting place was described as the "center of the universe." Signs placed in strategic locations told of a prohibition on singing and musical instruments. One sign said, "It is not necessary to give money to the *pir*, but your faith will be enhanced if you do." Perhaps one disciple had little cash and was in need of faith—for someone took fifteen dollars from my wallet.

The *pir* did not make an appearance during our time at the meeting. We understood that he would lead prayer at 3 A.M. He is about sixty years old and has two sons. His devotees worship him, while his critics consider him a corrupted religious leader who has turned Islam into a business venture. He initiates his disciples by pressing his finger into their chests just over the heart. At that time the devotee becomes filled with God and actually hears the voice of Allah within his body.

I talked to one retired army colonel and asked him why he was a follower of the *pir*. He told a long story of how he was tired of a materialistic orientation to life. More than anything else, he wanted peace and an experience with God. Contact with the *pir* had met his innermost longing for a personal encounter with the God of love.

At 1 A.M. we walked away from the teeming masses of simple, devout, questing Muslims. Our hearts ached that these misguided seekers of God might be introduced to the one who alone can fill hungry souls and satisfy longing hearts.

SUFISM IN CONFLICT

Is Sufism condoned in the Quran? Was Muhammad a mystic? Can there be a synthesis between orthodox Islam and Sufism? How serious is the breach between the two paths? These are serious questions that are occupying the minds of dedicated Muslim theologians on one hand and mystical practitioners on the other.

The early Sufis were said to have been orthodox Muslims in regard to their belief and practices. They put great emphasis on the teaching of the Quran and the Traditions. The distinctive features of their creed consisted of self-abandonment, self-mortification, and fervent piety.

It is interesting to read of one Muslim historian who has written, "According to all correct doctrines, then, the Quran is the first and the last textbook of Sufism, and the Prophet Muhammad the greatest Sufi of all times."[42] Another Muslim writer sees the basis for Sufism in the faith of the Prophet, who retired to the cave and received a mystical communication from God.[43]

> The esoteric teachings of the Quran and Hadith helped in the growth of ascetic and devotional tendencies. Hence it is an accomplished fact that Sufism originated under the lively influences of the Quran where references of Divine and mystical passages with esoteric meanings are to be found and also in the Hadith. A comparison between the orthodox tenets and Sufi doctrines will easily establish the theory. But the modern researchers have tried to show that the development of Sufism was due to a number of external factors. These non-Islamic influences which subsequently give a speculative and pantheistic character were moulded and recast in Islamic mystical inclinations. These are 1. Christianity, 2. Neo-Platonism, 3. Gnosticism, 4. Buddhism or Vedantism. Hence the theory that the origin of Sufism is purely un-Islamic is untenable, but it can be said that its development was fostered by foreign cultural influences.[44]

It is true that many ideas in the Quran afford a basis for Sufism. Although Muhammad's relation to God cannot on the whole be called one of intimacy, it had in it a mystical aspect, namely, a direct consciousness of God's presence. A list of some of his Quranic writings that indicate mysticism includes:

"Remember Me and I will remember you" (2:152).

"Call unto Me and I will answer you" (11:60).

"Wherever you turn there is the face of God" (2:115).

"A people whom He loveth and who love Him" (5:57).

"Those who love . . . and have a desire to seek the countenance of their Lord, Most High" (92:17, 20).

"Adore, and draw thou nigh" (96:19).

"We are from God and to God is our return" (2:156).

The Quran is said to possess two aspects, the exoteric and the esoteric. The former is meant for general readers while the latter is directed toward the "elect." The Quran is likened to a Rosetta stone which when deciphered will reveal inexhaustible treasures. So it was to the early Muslims who sought to be enlightened. They dedicated their time and effort to unraveling the hidden meanings of the Quran. This holy book thus is said to be the wellspring of Sufism.[45]

One of my scholarly Muslim friends makes a distinction between Islamic mysticism and Muslim mysticism. The former is that which is based on and can be substantiated by the Quran and Hadith. It is the mystical orientation to life that can be embraced by orthodox, practicing Muslims worldwide. There is no extremism or aberrant practices within this mysticism. All is explicitly or implicitly approved by the Holy Books of Islam. It allows for an individual's hunger for a relationship with a personal God but provides boundaries.

Muslim mysticism, on the other hand, is a pejorative term applied to Sufi practice that gives only superficial acknowledgment to Muhammad and the Quran, while allowing such anomalous activities as worshiping *pirs* or presenting gifts at shrines. An example of Muslim mysticism would be the behavior of a group of Sufis I watched who were projecting themselves as God-intoxicated people. After a prolonged session of singing esoteric-type Islamic songs, they proceeded to prepare *ganja* (a strong, mind-altering drug). At the proper moment, a devotee shouted, *"Bis-millah Rahmaner Rahim"*("In the name of God the beneficent and merciful"; it is blasphemy for an orthodox Muslim to utter these holy Arabic Quranic words in such a context) and then took a long puff on the water pipe in which the *ganja* had been placed. He immediately swooned and almost spilled the pipe onto the grass mat in the process. Others followed.

Muslim mysticism is man-made; that is, an interpretation and practice that is deviant from the Quran. Islamic mysticism is pure and true. The problem with these distinctions is the task of judging that which is erroneous. My experience is that five Muslims will have five views on the gray areas of Sufi practice. It is difficult, if not impossible, to construct an authoritative, widely acceptable, clear distinction between these two forms of mysticism.

As we have seen, at a point in early Muslim history there was a negative reaction against cold, rigid Islamic orthodoxy. Out of an emphasis on intellectualism and formalism by Muslim theologians came Sufi-type mysticism. Love became the Sufi byword. This, however, engendered a conflict.

> In fact, if the Sufi thinkers of India adhere to any religion, it is the religion of love. Indeed, they outwardly profess theological Islam as their religion, but their conception of Islam is different, in many fundamental respects, from the conception of Muslim theologians. The Islam they profess to honor is more of their own creation than of the creation of the Quran. All the formalities of Islam, its code of law *(shariat)*, its teachings and morals as inculcated by the doctors of Islam *(imams)* have been set aside, and in their places, they have installed their own formalities, laws, teachings, and morals. They have interpreted the Quran and the Traditions (Hadith) in their own light.[46]

The Sufi outlook is said to take a rather negative or otherworldly view of life. Islam is more positive, saying a firm yes to life. Anwar Ali comments that "this difference is fundamental, and it is no mere accident that popular beliefs in the Sufi cults coincided with the decadence of the Muslim community."[47]

An important area of conflict concerns the personal versus social orientation of Sufis and orthodox Muslims. Islam is to be concerned with the community as a whole and views life in both its spiritual and temporal aspects. It seeks a balance between indulgence and asceticism. To the mystic, however, the personal experience is supremely important. His whole life is wrapped up in his quest for God. He gives little thought to the needs of the community.

It is interesting to read of the mystical orientation toward the Prophet that developed among Sufis. Nicholson, one of the world's renowned scholars on Sufism, has researched the subject:

> During the Middle Ages the person of Muhammad stands in the very center of the mystical life of Islam. Abu Hasan al-Hirali, a Sufi of the 13th century, describes three kinds of faith in the Prophet. The third and highest kind is peculiar to those in reference to whom God hath said, "Heaven and earth contain Me not, but the heart of my believing servant containeth Me." They love one another in God and are the vicegerents of God in the world. Their faith consists in the belief that when the Prophet ascended to heaven he received of God's Word (amr) that which is hidden from all the prophets and angels and from Gabriel himself. None of the holy spirits and cherubim ever enjoyed such a Divine Revelation as was bestowed on Muhammad. And faith in Muhammad is the measure of one's faith in God. The only way to God is through faith in Muhammad.[48]

It has been a source of amazement to me to see how tolerant the orthodox Muslim is of Sufism. Generally the two coexist with little more than verbal critiques of each other's view. Each, of course, feels his position to be superior. The law-based fundamentalist is convinced his allegiance to the Quran and the Traditions is total. There can be no other method of knowing God except through the ritual as prescribed in the Holy Books.

Any experience-seeking devotee of God will be led into deviation and excess. Meanwhile, the Sufi stares in disbelief at the law-bound Muslim. How can such cold ritual lead to knowing God? The only path is to experience the warm emotion of love and eventual assimilation into God. This is reality! Liberty, faith, absorption—these are to be the dynamics operative in the life of a seeker of God.

There is one very vocal opponent to Sufism. Saudi Arabia has never been able to support a mysticism that is outside a rigid interpretation of the Quran and the Traditions. Therefore, Saudis categorize what they find in the subcontinent as un-Islamic. Their ambassador in one of the countries of the subcontinent goes throughout the land holding various meetings in which he appeals to the Muslim citizenry to return to the fold of true Islam. He vehemently denounces the *pir* system and other deviations that he, from his fundamentalist perspective, finds abhorrent. His appeals fall on deaf ears.

So, one concludes, Sufism is here to stay. It has no plans to launch crusades against orthodoxy. Its quiet work of person-to-person propagation will continue—just as it has for at least one thousand years.

NOTES

1. Thelma Sioson-San Juan, "Mt. Banahaw: a world rooted in religion," Manila *Times Journal* (June 24, 1981), 4.
2. Jaime Bulatao, "The New Mysticism in the Philippine Church," Manila *Bulletin Today* (June 23, 1981), 6.
3. Quoted in Aziz Ahmad, *Studies in Islamic Culture in the Indian Environment* (Oxford: Clarendon, 1964), 119.
4. Kenneth Cragg, *Sandals at the Mosque* (London; SCM, 1959), 80.
5. Fadlou Shehadi, *Ghazali's Unique Unknowable God* (Leiden: Brill, 1964), 22.
6. A. J. Arberry, *Sufism: An Account of the Mystics of Islam* (London: George Allen and Unwin, 1950), 35.

7. Idries Shah, *The Way of the Sufi* (New York: Dutton, 1970), 222.

8. John A. Subhan, *Sufism: Its Saints and Shrines* (Lucknow: Lucknow Publishing House, 1938), 6.

9. Violet Rhoda Jones and L. Bevan Jones, *Woman in Islam* (Lucknow: Lucknow Publishing House, 1941), 300.

10. Reynold A. Nicholson, "Mysticism," in *The Legacy of Islam*, ed. Sir Thomas Arnold and Alfred Guillaume (London: Oxford University, 1949), 233.

11. Edwin Elliot Calverly, *Worship in Islam, being a translation with commentary and introduction of Al-Ghazzali's Book of the Ihya on the Worship* (Madras: Christian Literature Society for India, 1925), 82.

12. Wilfred Cantwell Smith, *Islam in Modern History* (New York: New American Library, Mentor Books, 1957), 44–45.

13. Muhammad Enamul Haq, *A History of Sufi-ism in Bengal* (Dacca: Asiatic Society of Bangladesh, 1975), 89.

14. Arberry, *Sufism*, 45.

15. Idries Shah, *Oriental Magic* (Tonbridge, England: Octagon Press, 1968), vii.

16. Anwarul Karim, *The Bauls of Bangladesh* (Kushtia: Lalon Academy, 1980), 64.

17. Subhan, *Sufism: Its Saints and Shrines*, 11.

18. Nicholson, "Mysticism," 213.

19. Arberry, *Sufism*, 67.

20. S. M. Hasan, *Muslim Creed and Culture* (Dacca: Ideal Publications, 1962), 300–301.

21. Karim, *The Bauls of Bangladesh*, 117.

22. Ahmad, *Studies in Islamic Culture*, 121–122.

23. Peter G. Gowing and William Henry Scott, *Acculturation in the Philippines* (Quezon City: New Day Publishers, 1971), 12.

24. Ibid., 14.

25. Ikbal Ali, *Islamic Sufism* (Delhi: Idarah-i Adabiyat-i Delli, 1933), 292.

26. Haq, *History of Sufi-ism in Bengal*, 21.

27. Ahmad, *Studies in Islamic Culture*, 83.

28. Haq, *History of Sufi-ism in Bengal*, 261.

29. Karim, *The Bauls of Bangladesh*, 55–56.

30. Lajwanti Rama Krishna, *Punjabi Sufi Poets* A.D. *1460–1900* (Karachi: Indus Publishers, 1977), 134.

31. Ahmad, *Studies in Islamic Culture*, 166.

32. S. Q. Fatemi, *Islam Comes to Malaysia*, ed. Shirli Gordon (Singapore: Malaya Publishing House, 1963), 94.

33. Cesar Adib Majul, *Muslims in the Philippines* (Quezon City: University of the Philippines, 1973), 49.

34. Mamitua Saber and Abdullah T. Madale, eds., *The Maranao* (Manila: Solidaridad Publishing House, 1975), 31.

35. David W. Shenk, "The [Sufi] Mystical Orders in Popular Islam" (unpublished paper, 1981), 1.

36. Haq, *History of Sufi-ism in Bengal*, 36.

37. Quoted in Subhan, *Sufism: Its Saints and Shrines*, 215.

38. Ibid., 230.

39. Ibid., 233.

40. Ibid., 255.

41. Ibid., 279.

42. Ali, *Islamic Sufism*, 14.

43. Karim, *The Bauls of Bangladesh*, 63.

44. Hasan, *Muslim Creed and Culture*, 397.

45. Syed Naguib al Atlas, *Some Aspects of Sufism as Understood and Practised Among the Malays* (Singapore: Malaya Publishing House, 1963), 4.

46. Haq, *History of Sufi-ism in Bengal*, 88.

47. Anwar Ali, *Islam: Ideology and Leading Issues* (Lahore: Publishers United, 1978), 147.

48. Reynold A. Nicholson, *The Idea of Personality in Sufism* (1923; reprinted Delhi: Idarah-i Adabiyat-i Delli, 1976), 63.

2

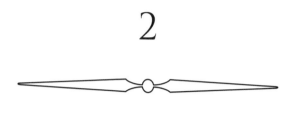

SUFI BELIEF

An excellent, succinct summary of Sufi belief has been written by Thomas P. Hughes:

> God exists. He is in all things, and all things are in Him.
>
> All visible and invisible beings are an emanation from Him, and are not really distinct from Him.
>
> Religions are matters of indifference: they however serve as leading to realities. Some for this purpose are more advantageous than others, among which is Islam, of which Sufism is the true philosophy.
>
> There does not really exist any difference between good and evil, for all is reduced to Unity, and God is the real Author of the acts of mankind.
>
> It is God who fixes the will of man: man therefore is not free in his actions.
>
> The soul existed before the body and is confined within the latter as in a cage. Death, therefore, should be the object of the wishes of the Sufi, for it is then that he returns to the bosom of Divinity.
>
> Without the Grace of God no one can attain to spiritual union, but this can be obtained by fervently asking for it.

The principal occupation of the Sufi while in the body is meditation on the unity of God, the remembrance of God's names, and the progressive advancement in the journey of life so as to attain unification with God.[1]

PIRS AND SHRINES

One of the most controversial aspects of Sufism is the activity of a select fraternity of spiritual guides known as *pirs*. These men are said to be endued with special powers that are transmittable to *murids* (followers). *Pirs* are basically mediators between God and man. Orthodox Islam forcefully rejects a system that elevates a man to a position wherein he almost becomes god in the eyes of his followers. Islamic fundamentalists decry what they perceive as a personality cult. They see the *pirs* detracting attention from God and focusing it on themselves. Also, they declare the financial dealings of the *pir* to be suspect.

Synonymous with the word *pir* is the noun *saint*. The word for saint, *awliya,* literally means "friend." Saints are regarded as God's special friends. They are the elect of the Sufis. Their biographies, miracles, and teachings, and the legends about them are studied and passed on by oral tradition from generation to generation. Sufis of every class invoke their names in hours of distress.

It is for the *pir* to win the favor of men through his holy way of living or through the performance of a miraculous deed. He might also claim the status of a *pir* by solving a mystery of life. His esoteric knowledge of God gives him the dignity and respect necessary to gather a group of devotees.

The *pir* should be worthy of imitation. He should have a perfect knowledge, both theoretical and practical, of the stages of the mystical life. He should also be entirely purged of fleshly urges so that nothing of his lower self remains in him.[2]

Reynold A. Nicholson further writes of the stages involved in becoming a saint:

Asceticism and positive religion are thus relegated to the lower planes of the mystical life. The Sufi needs them and must hold fast to them while he is serving his spiritual apprenticeship and also during the middle stage which is marked by longer or shorter intervals of illumination; but in his last "state," when the unveiling is completed, he has no further use for ascetic practices and religious forms, for he lives in permanent communion with God Himself. This leads directly to antinomianism, though in theory the saint is above the law rather than against it.[3]

Mahatma Gandhi, the famous Indian statesman, was mystically oriented. During the last year of his life he went to the district of Noakhali in Bangladesh seeking to bring peace and stability to the seething problems that existed between the Hindu and Muslim communities. In his company was a young, attractive female—a distant relative who acted as his attendant-cum-companion. Gandhi created a sensation around the world when word was leaked that he and the young woman were sleeping together in the nude. The great old man of India couldn't understand all the commotion. He was only proving to himself that he had passed beyond sexual desire and that he could sleep in proximity to temptation without experiencing fleshly lust. He felt he needed this assurance of becoming one with God before embracing death. In light of the stir caused in the non-mystical world, Gandhi declared himself pure—and proceeded to live separately from the young woman!

The *pir*, having established his reputation as a man of special power, begins to recruit disciples from among those who come to him. This relationship resembles that of a Hindu and his *guru* (Hindu spiritual guide). It is to be understood that no one can become a Sufi without being initiated as a follower of a *pir*. This is the door into Sufism. So it is right and proper to ask each person who claims to be a Sufi who his *pir* is. From the answer received the path or *tarika* is understood. One then can have a fair grasp of what the individual Sufi's beliefs are.

The rite of initiation is most interesting.

The *pir* is believed to be able to "transmit" spiritual power to his *murid*. This he does by the exercise of *"tawajjuh"* or "concentration." When a *pir* desires to exercise *tawajjuh* on one of his disciples, he seats himself near him and proceeds in imagination to picture his own heart as in close proximity to that of his *murid*, at the same time concentrating his mind upon the idea that his power is now being transmitted from his own heart to that of the other. At the same time the *murid* is required to concentrate his mind on the idea that he is receiving the power from his *pir*. This rite is generally performed at the time when the *pir*, after the performance of the *dhikr*, is in an abnormal state of mind.[4]

I had the opportunity to observe a *pir* induct a group of followers into his order. Some three thousand people had gathered to be a part of the annual event. There was a fair-like atmosphere. In one corner a group of long-haired youth was playing one-string banjos and singing praises to God in esoteric symbolic lyrics. In a large field, hundreds of men, women, and children were eating rice and curry which was being served to them on banana leaves. Scores of small stores had opened along the sides of the meeting area. Men were sitting around gossiping and eating, quite oblivious to the preaching that was blaring from a loudspeaker. The Muslim preachers were giving simple exhortations to the faithful to live pure lives. Their messages were punctuated with stories that caused great laughter among the several hundred devotees seated in the open on bamboo mats. The speakers would frequently urge the audience to stay awake—an exhortation that often fell upon sleeping ears. From time to time, the men giving messages would switch to a chanting mode of delivery. This seemed to be greatly appreciated.

At one point in the meeting, the volume of the microphone was lowered and the Muslims who were to be initiated were told to meet the *pir* in one corner of the courtyard. Shortly thereafter, an aged man with a humpback (devotees believe this *pir* to be more than 120 years old) appeared on the veranda of a house. His movements were deliberate and his voice muted. The *pir* began giving exhortations from the Quran regarding the necessity of following God. The one hundred soon-to-be-initiated disciples listened in rapt attention.

An assistant brought a very long, narrow piece of cloth which was passed from person to person. The object was for each devotee to have his hand on the cloth, which was held on one end by the *pir*. At this point, the *pir* had everyone stand while he prayed that God would forgive each one's sins. In this act could be seen the mediatorial role of the *pir*. Spiritual power was being transmitted from the *pir* to those being initiated. The bond was symbolized by the cloth that was being touched by all present.

The next function was similar in purpose. A glass of lemonade was brought to the *pir*. He first breathed into it. (It is a common practice among Sufis for a man of spiritual power to breathe on a sick person or on some object.) This puff of air from within the *pir's* body is said to contain power from God. Next, the *pir* put his finger in the glass of lemonade and then touched his finger to his tongue. Then he dipped his finger again into the glass. This was repeated three times.

The lemonade was then poured into a large pitcher. Assistants took the container and walked among the crowd to give each devotee a small glass of the empowered drink. All were most anxious to receive their share. This drink which had been sanctified by the *pir* was a further tangible expression of the transmission of spiritual power from saint to disciples. Lastly, all stood while the *pir* prayed. Following this, the new initiates lined up in front of a clerk who received and duly recorded their financial contribution to the *pir* for the ensuing year.

In fact, the *pir* becomes a little god. He is to be followed in blind faith. In one sense, the *pir* is a present substitute for the departed Prophet Muhammad. The least word of a *pir* is absolute law to the disciple. Even if the *pir's* commands contravene the letter of the law, they must be fulfilled. Such is the overwhelming power of saint over devotee. The pact between saint and disciple can never be dissolved unilaterally by the will of the devotee.

Many *pirs* claim their lineage can be traced back to the Prophet. Thus, their authority is total and not subject to question.

> As for initiation in Sufism, this consists in the transmission of a spiritual influence (*barakah*) and must be conferred by a representative of a "chain" reaching back to the Prophet. In most cases it is transmitted by the master who also communicates the method and confers the means of spiritual concentration that are appropriate to the aptitudes of the disciple.[5]

The Persian word *pir* means "old man." An interesting counterpart is the Buddhist word *therea*, which has the same meaning. Buddhists had a practice called *chaitya-puja*, which denotes worship at the graves of saintly old men. The Buddhists attributed mysterious power to their *thereas*. Therefore, they did not burn their bodies, but rather buried them and built special shrines over the graves. Then the Buddhists sprinkled perfume around the area of the shrine. Offerings of food and flowers were also placed within the shrine.

Muhammad Enamul Haq has commented on the syncretism that took place between Buddhism and Islam:

> Undoubtedly, when Buddhist Turks and other people were converted to Islam in the eleventh and twelfth centuries, they introduced their old practices and beliefs to Islam under new names. Though they kept everything intact, yet *therea* became *pir* and *dhupa, dhuna,* sandalpaste, lotus flowers etc. were subsequently replaced by *luban, liar,* and *gulab. Chaitya puja* was current in Bengal as in other lands where Buddhism flourished. The descendants of *Chaitya* worshipers, when converted to Islam, became saint worshipers.[6]

Today at the graves of saints one sees offerings of flowers, vermilion, and other articles that are used in the Hindu *pujas* or worship ceremonies. In the next chapter, I will describe in some detail the very colorful (as well as very un-Islamic) practices that are carried out at these shrines.

It is important to understand the rationale for such worship. The purpose is not just to show respect for departed saints. That would be permissible within orthodox Islam. However, the worship that takes place at shrines throughout the Muslim world has as its purpose the attaining of supernatural help for the devotee through the ongoing intercessory assistance of the departed *pir.* There is believed to be a special power present at the shrine. By presenting offerings, the disciple can make petitions to God through the mediatorial efforts of the saint. I am not an expert on Roman Catholicism, but it would seem that the Catholic view on departed saints through whom prayer is offered to God is a parallel to Sufi saint worship.

Often the activities of saints are lost in antiquity. There then builds up an apocryphal folk history concerning these *pirs.* The stories related in chapter 1 are examples. The disciples of any departed saint feel obligated to make his activities appear as significant as possible. This is done with little regard for the ethics of being truthful.

Sufism would not exist without living *pirs* as well as dead *pirs.* They are the keys that unlock Sufi doctrine and point the way to progression through the various stages of spiritual development.

MYSTICAL STAGES

Sufism is open to the charge that it is pantheistic, an issue that Nicholson has sought to clarify:

> The development of Sufi pantheism comes much later than Hallaj and was chiefly due to Ibmul-Arabi (A.D. 1165–1240). It would be a mistake to suppose that utterances like the Subhani, "Glory to me," of Bayazid, the Anal-Haqq, "I am God," of Hallaj, and the Ana Hiya, "I am She," of Ibnul-Farid are in themselves evidence of pantheism. So long as transcendence is recognized, the most emphatic assertion of immanence is not pantheism but panentheism—not the doctrine that all is God, but the doctrine that all is in God, who is also above all.[7]

Another author has described Sufi belief by stating, "If the Creator and the created are one, the created may claim godhead. Then the natural conclusion that follows is that there is nothing in the universe which is not a God."[8] The issue will become a bit clearer by a consideration of the stages through which the devoted Sufi passes. It is essential to grasp the importance of these stages.

1. The Sufi is exhorted to serve God as the initial step toward a knowledge of Him. This is the first stage of his journey, and is called *ubudiyah* or service. At this point the aspiring Sufi looks for the opportunity to assist or offer hospitality to others. Several times I have had food almost forced upon me as the Sufis felt they could not let me leave their presence without receiving something from their hand. "Who makes his soul mature in the service of God and makes his heart habituated with good works and good activities, becomes accustomed to avoiding the worldly pleasures, and gets full control over lusts and desires, he it is who attains the position of nearness to God."[9]

2. *Ishq,* or love of God, is the second stage. "It is here especially that the emotional character of Sufism, so different from the cold theories of the Indian philosophies, is apparent. Love here as with so many of the mystics in all ages and all countries, is the Sovereign Alchemy, transmuting the base metal of humanity into the Divine God."[10] At this point the mystic may write songs that express his love to God. He will seek out the companionship of other like-minded individuals. They will attend musical functions that are centered around the worship and praising of God.

3. A more ascetic outlook on life is developed in the third stage, which is known as *zuhd* or seclusion. The Sufi may retreat from all worldly cares and seek to meditate on God in an effort to come to know Him more intimately.

4. These contemplations and investigations of metaphysical theories concerning the nature, attributes, and works of God lead to *marifah* or knowledge. "The great object of the Sufi is to escape from the trammels of humanity, and return to the bosom of divinity, while the teachings of their mystic creed are supposed to lead the soul onward, stage by stage, until it reaches the goal of perfect knowledge."[11] It is

common for a Sufi to identify his order as *Marifahti*. In reality this is not one's order, but a stage of spiritual development within an order. In common usage the term designates a Sufi who is in quest of the knowledge of God. The Sufi's mystical orientation to life will be apparent from his manner of speaking as well as his behavior.

5. As a result of meditation on and contemplation of God, the Sufi is introduced to a state of mental excitement known as *wajd* or ecstasy. This stage is a definite indication that the Sufi has received direct illumination from God. The more emotional Eastern seeker of God especially enjoys this stage of enlightenment. As will be seen, *dhikr* (a ceremony that focuses on the recitation of the names and attributes of God) leads to a frenzy of emotion especially enjoyed by Sufis in this stage.

6. *Haqiqah,* or truth, is the stage when the seeker receives a revelation of the true nature of the godhead. It is also a time when the Sufi may boldly identify himself as the truth. To assist the reader in understanding the implications of this stage, the following widely accepted biographical sketch of Al-Hallaj is presented.

> When al-Junaid in this way was succeeding to escape from the mortal peril of preaching the apotheosis of man, his junior contemporary, Al-Hallaj, was not so fortunate in his reading of the riddle of existence, and being condemned for blasphemy he was executed upon the cross in 922. He went along with al-Junaid so far as seeing in the supreme mystical experience a reunion with God; but he then proceeded further and taught that man may thus be viewed as very God incarnate, taking as his example not, as one might suppose, Muhammad, but Jesus. He did not claim Divinity for himself; though the utterance which led to his execution, "I am the Truth," seemed to his judges to have that implication. The context of this startling paradox occurs in his *Kitab al-Tawasin,*
>
> > If ye do not recognize God, at least recognize His sign. I am the Creative Truth, because through the Truth I am a truth eternally. My friends and teachers are Iblis and Pharaoh.

Iblis was threatened by Hell-fire, yet he did not recant. Pharaoh was drowned in the sea, yet he did not recant, for he would not acknowledge anything between him and God. And I, though I am killed and crucified, and though my hands and feet are cut off—I do not recant.

When he was brought to be crucified and saw the cross and nails, he turned to the people and uttered a prayer, ending with the words: "And these Thy servants who are gathered to slay me, in zeal for Thy religion and in desire to win Thy favor, forgive them, O Lord, and have mercy upon them; for verily if Thou hadst revealed to them that which Thou hast revealed to me, they would not have done what they have done; and if Thou hadst hidden from me that which Thou hast hidden from them, I should not have suffered this tribulation! Glory unto Thee in whatsoever Thou doest, and glory unto Thee in whatsoever Thou willest."[12]

In the tenth century, orthodox Islam was unwilling to deal leniently with such heresy. Al-Hallaj was prepared to suffer a horrible death rather than recant. Sufis, in retrospect, regard Al-Hallaj as a very special saint. Fundamental Islam declares him a heretic who was justly punished.

7. *Wasl* or union with God, is the last stage of enlightenment for the Sufi. At this point the Sufi no longer is just a man, but is transubstantiated into God. He then declares, *"Ana-l-haqq"* (I am the real). This utterance is blasphemous to the orthodox Muslim. To Sufis, the person who attains the seventh stage possesses a spiritual superiority. "Arguments are generally advanced in his favor with the explanation that he who can utter such a seeming blasphemy, is not really blasphemous; for, it is not the utterance of a man of flesh and blood, but the utterance of the Real, through the man, i.e., the utterance of the Infinite through the finite."[13]

Mystical poetry identifies this stage of assimilation into God as a completely blissful state of mind. No pain is felt. A mystic loses his individual entity in the fathomless ocean of God. Just as a word is inseparable from its meaning, an eye from its sight, and a flower from its fragrance, so also is the Sufi inseparable from his Beloved. He is now no longer a man who obeys, but a highly developed spiritual person who is obeyed by others. In this state his utterances and actions are not his own, but those of God Himself.

At the end of the eighth century, Abu Yazid professed to reach this stage. Some of his statements included, "Beneath this cloak of mine there is nothing but God." "Glory to me! How great is my majesty!" "Verily I am God; there is no god beside me, so worship me!"[14]

The Sufi can go no further than this. During the remainder of his life he pursues the art of contemplation. Death is regarded as *fana* or total absorption into God.

Adherents of a parallel school of thought are known as theistic mystics. These devotees claim to be within the mainstream of Islam and reject the excessive teachings that lead one to say he has become God.

> The Theist mystics do not speak of union with God, but illumination from God or closeness to God. They hold that even when the mystic passes away from his individual will and enters into the Divine Will so that all his life is devoted entirely to God, his ego still remains intact. Even when in ecstasy he loses his senses he is aware of this loss of senses as a distinct ego. There are moments when the ego-consciousness also seems to disappear, but actually it is still there; it is only momentarily outshone by the Divine vision, as the light of the stars is outshone by the light of the sun. These moments rapidly pass away, and the ego-consciousness appears again.[15]

One can see the parallels of this mystical experience and that of the Christian who is also seeking illumination and closeness to God. The follower of Christ mystically speaks of God dwelling in him and of being possessed of the Holy Spirit, but he does not go on to the excesses of Sufism in which the ultimate experience is to become God.

Few Sufis claim to reach the seventh stage. If they do attain this state, they will be famous and will have a huge following. Most Sufis are happy to reach the fourth stage. This indicates that they are in search of mystical truth and sets them apart as persons seriously in pursuit of God.

TEACHINGS AND PRACTICES OF MYSTICS

Several subjects are considered important in Sufism. There will not be uniform agreement on belief and practice by all mystics on each of these points. This overview, however, will describe the generally accepted view rather than the anomalous.

TERMINOLOGY

The uninitiated will not understand the terminology of the Sufis. The concept of mystery is important to the mystic. He desires to possess something of value and uniqueness that no one else has. His uniqueness is expressed on a metaphysical and linguistic level. He portrays his love and devotion to God in esoteric terminology. These words may even have sexual or fertility connotations that the non-mystic is completely unaware of.

For example, the word *perfume* may signify sleep or meditation; the term *wine* refers to devotion. The Sufis often speak of having drunk wine to the point of insensibility (this is to be understood as devotional ecstasy rather than drunkenness caused by the consumption of an alcoholic beverage); the Sufi is now under the total influence of God. A tavern is the place of prayer. The tavernkeeper is the spiritual leader or the *pir.* The word *beauty* refers to the perfection of God.

> The metaphysical terminology of the Sufis is largely derived from the Quran: in expressions like "fire" for the purity of God, "bird" as a symbol of the resurrection or immortality of the human soul, "tree" as the symbol representing the destiny and vocation of man, the wine and the cup are used for initiation into Sufi orders and thence borrowed from Arabic, Persian, Turkish, and Urdu poetry.[16]

The word *God* is not quickly spoken, but rather gradually approached through various so-called revelations. One of the first words used for

God is "existence." This is followed by the name *one.* The more the descriptive word particularizes, the higher on the scale it is. When the mystic finally reaches the word *Allah,* the intensity of the illumination is such as to almost overwhelm him.

DHIKR

The importance of words—and particularly the name of Allah—is seen in a unique and fascinating ceremony called *dhikr.*

> We enter a dimly-lighted room where a number of men are gathered. As we do so a signal is given by a man who appears to be the leader of the assembly and the doors are shut. There is a hush as twelve men form into two parallel lines in the center of the room. The glimmer of a solitary hurricane lamp falls on the dark faces in which only eyes seem to live. The rest of us fall back to the sides of the room. The *dhikr* is about to begin. With a startling clap of the hands the leader starts swaying from right to left. Very slowly he begins, and the men fall into the rhythm of his swaying. Every time they sway to the left, they call "Hu!" in chorus. "Hu . . . Hu . . . Hu. . . ." So the monotonous chant proceeds with at first hardly any perceptible increase in tempo. But gradually the movement of their bodies becomes more rapid and the sound of "Hu! Hu! Hu!" comes faster and faster with a crescendo corresponding with the quicker time. At last the excitement becomes so intense that a man there, and a boy here, slip to their knees, still swaying in unison with the others till finally they fall and collapse on the floor. One man goes forward and looks at the faces of these two and leaves them where they lie. Thus course after course of this chanting and swaying beginning from the slower and proceeding to the wild orgy of motion and shouting, proceeds according to the leader's direction, who brings the whole course to its end by a loud shout of "Hu!" and a wild jerk to the left. Then dead silence prevails, succeeded by the low undertone of prayer in which all who have not fallen unconscious join.[17]

The word *dhikr* means "remembrance." Sufis have built the ceremony of *dhikr* on an interpretation of a verse that constantly recurs in the Quran: "Remember God often." Actually the verse has an obvious meaning free from any interpretation that could lead devotees into an excess of emotionalism.

Dhikr is commonly practiced among Muslims of all schools of thought. However, excessive emotional frenzy would be repudiated by the orthodox. The aim of *dhikr* is to block out all worldly distractions and become completely absorbed in thinking about God.

Dhikr can focus on more than just the name Allah. The attributes and the ninety-nine names of God are frequently chanted in *dhikr* fashion. Each of the names is emotionally repeated twenty to thirty times before the participants go on to the next in the series.

Sufis believe that "the performance of *dhikr* as prescribed by the *murshid* (spiritual guide) can save the man from the evils of the flesh *(nafs)* and lead him to the ultimate goal of union with God."[18] Therefore, *dhikr* is a vehicle that moves the devotee away from sin and to holiness.

THE QURAN AND MUHAMMAD

The word *tilawat* refers to the reciting of the Quran. In *tilawat,* both the Sufi and the orthodox Muslim believe they are pronouncing the very words of Allah as dictated to the Prophet Muhammad. Every word of the Quran is inerrant and above critical investigation. It is to be accepted by faith. The Sufi, on hearing these words, believes he is hearing the very sound of the Beloved of his soul. As a result of such a belief, the mystic is often thrown into a state of ecstasy while just reading the Quran—or hearing it read. Thus, for Sufis whose religious orders forbid the use of music as a means of inducing the state of ecstasy, the reading or chanting of the Quran takes its place.

There continues to be a conflict in Islam between the importance of the Quran on one hand and poems and songs on the other. Sufis feel comfortable with all of these.

To a Muslim the Arabic Quran is the sublime word of God, but the mystic song speaks in a language that is easily understood, for it speaks in terms of love and appeals to the deepest emotion. It rouses in his heart the innermost longing for union with God. This is what led Dr. Pusey to observe that the speedy growth of mystical doctrine in the thin and arid soil of Muhammadanism also bears eloquent witness to the longing innate in the human heart for union with God.[19]

The mystics' view of the Prophet Muhammad is not uniform. To highlight this conflict of views I want to present the opinions of Nicholson as contrasted with those of Haq.

Nicholson states that devotion to the Prophet is often expressed in esoteric language within Sufi hymns and poetry. Muhammad is the "Beloved of God" and therefore the Beloved of all Sufis. Some claim mystical union with him, of "passing away" *(fana)* in him. It is inadequate only to imitate his actions and qualities. His living presence is longed for. Muhammad is said by some to assume the form of a saint and is revered as such by the initiated. A large number of Sufis claim that the Prophet appears to them very often in dreams. These visions are momentous and create a significant impact on the life of the devotee.

Sufis also believe, according to Nicholson, in Muhammad's intercessory role. The Prophet will make intercession on the day of resurrection during the time of judgment. Sufis claim this assistance from Muhammad as part of their heritage.[20]

Haq confines his comments to the Sufis of the Indian subcontinent. He takes the view that allegiance to the Prophet is more semantic than real.

> The position of the Prophet is somewhat awkward in Islam among Indian Sufis. We have mentioned before that they claim a direct relation with God. There is no question that the Prophet has fallen in the background owing to this direct relation. Indian Sufis certainly admit the prophethood of Muhammad, but from the practical point of view, his position is not so glorious and exalted to them as that of a *murshid*

or a *pir*. However much a direct relation they establish between God and man, they cannot do away with the idea of an intermediary like *murshid* who has practically usurped the intermediary and intercessionary functions of the Prophet who thus being deprived of these two important functions, has really been reduced to a mere figurehead only to hoodwink the orthodox.[21]

It is my view that both Nicholson and Haq are correct. Sufism is never uniform. One *tarika* would give teaching that presents identification with Muhammad as an ultimate mystical experience. Another group would give lip service to the position and honor of the Prophet, but in reality replace him with its *pir*. It is important to note that few if any Sufis would openly attack the Quran or the Prophet. They may strongly react against the law as presented in the Quran and Hadith, but in their minds this is a very indirect criticism and not one of significant offense. They would say that the Quran advocates a personal relationship with God and that is the really important thing in life.

EXPERIENCE AND AUSTERITY

Mystics can point with pride to theologians, writers, and poets. Yet, by and large the academic side of Sufism is submerged in a sea of subjectivity. Experience is the important thing in life. Sufis thoroughly enjoy "doing their own thing." One would never charge a Sufi with being eccentric. The range of acceptable behavior is too broad to allow for such a charge.

Devotees are pressured to continue to seek a deeper experience with God. One Sufi writer urged disciples to "die to self and live to God." This dying to self is called *al-Junaid fana,* a term reminiscent of the Quranic phrase, "Everything is perishing except His face." The term does not mean that the mystic literally ceases to exist. Rather his individuality is perfected and eternalized through God.[22]

Islam has produced no less frequently than Christendom men who combine intense spiritual illumination with creative energy and aptitude for affairs on a grand scale. The

Mohammedan notion of the saint as a person possessed by God allows a very wide application of the term: in popular usage it extends from the greatest Sufi theosophists, like Jalalud-Din Rumi and Ibn al' Arabi, down to those who have gained sanctity only by losing sanity—victims of epilepsy and hysteria, half-witted idiots and harmless lunatics.[23]

Love and experiential religion, to a Sufi, are what life is all about. However, the emphasis on the vertical dimension of seeking and knowing God often causes a neglect of the horizontal dimension of showing concern for one's neighbor. The mystic is criticized for "being so heavenly minded he is no earthly good." *Dhikr* and meditation are often regarded as more important than earning a living.

Mystics are prone to asceticism. Their present worldly existence is evidence of a temporary separation from God. They must prepare for a permanent union with the Beloved. Every possible care must be taken for the development of the soul. The body is considered a prison from which one must escape. The evils of the flesh must be overcome through self-deprivation, physical hardship, and mental discipline.

Wandering mystics with long hair, unwashed bodies, and ragged clothes are more respected than pitied. They have set their sights on a heavenly city. Such Sufis are in pursuit of that which liberates and endures. The world with all its allurements and fleshly attractions has dimmed in the glaring light that proceeds from the very throne of God directly to the heart of the devotee who has forsaken all in order that he might come to fully know his Lord.

A poem by the famous thirteenth-century Persian poet Jalalud-Din Rumi brings Sufism into perspective:

> We have lost our heart in the way of the Beloved:
> We have sown dissension in the world.
> We have struck fire within the hearts of the people:
> And have thrown lovers into confusion.
> I have washed my hands of all my belongings:
> We have set fire to house and home.
> I had a heavy load on my back

But thanks be to God, we have thrown aside that heavy
load.

What is the wealth of the world but carrion?
We have cast the carcass to the dogs.
We have extracted the kernel of the Quran:
And the husk we have cast to the dogs.
We have scattered the seed of eternal felicity and joy
From the earth to the sky.

The patched robe [of the *darwish*], the prayer carpet and
the rosary,
We have cast away in the Tavern of Souls.

The pious cloak and turban and the babbling of
knowledge about jot and tittle,
We have thrown it all into the flowing stream.
From the bow of desire, the arrow of Gnosis,
Taking straight aim, we have shot at the target.
Thou hast well said O Shams-i-Tabriz,
We have cast love glances at the Lord of the Soul.[24]

NOTES

1. Thomas P. Hughes, *A Dictionary of Islam* (London: W. H. Allen, 1895), 609.

2. Reynold A. Nicholson, *Studies in Islamic Mysticism* (Cambridge: At the University Press, 1921), 22.

3. Ibid., 63.

4. John A. Subhan, *Sufism: Its Saints and Shrines* (Lucknow: Lucknow Publishing House, 1938), 88.

5. Titus Burckhardt, *An Introduction to Sufi Doctrine*, trans. D. M. Matheson (Lahore: Shaikh Muhammad Ashraf, 1959), 9.

6. Muhammad Enamul Haq, *A History of Sufi-ism in Bengal* (Dacca: Asiatic Society of Bangladesh, 1975), 324–325.

7. Reynold A. Nicholson, *The Idea of Personality in Sufism* (1923; reprinted Delhi: Idarah-i Adabiyat-i Delli, 1976), 27.

8. Haq, *History of Sufi-ism in Bengal*, 69.

9. Mustafa Halimi Pasha, *Tarikh-i-Tasawwuf-i-Islam*, trans. Rayees Ahmad Jafri (Lahore: n.p., 1950), 242.

10. Edward G. Browne, *A Literary History of Persia*, vol. 1, *From the Earliest Times until Firdawsi* (New York: Cambridge University, 1951), 441–442.

11. Thomas P. Hughes, *Notes on Muhammadanism*, 3d ed. (London: W. H. Allen, 1894), 228.

12. A. J. Arberry, *Sufism: An Account of the Mystics of Islam* (London: George Allen and Unwin, 1950), 59–60.

13. Haq, *History of Sufi-ism in Bengal*, 90.

14. Subhan, *Sufism: Its Saints and Shrines*, 21.

15. M. M. Sharif, *Muslim Thought: Its Origin and Achievements* (Lahore: Shaikh Muhammad Ashraf, 1951), 73–74.

16. Aziz Ahmad, *Studies in Islamic Culture in the Indian Environment* (Oxford: Clarendon, 1964), 120.

17. Subhan, *Sufism: Its Saints and Shrines*, 1–2.

18. Haq, *History of Sufi-ism in Bengal*, 101.

19. Subhan, *Sufism: Its Saints and Shrines*, 322–323.

20. Nicholson, *Idea of Personality in Sufism*, 64–66.

21. Haq, *History of Sufi-ism in Bengal*, 116–117.

22. Arberry, *Sufism: An Account of the Mystics of Islam*, 58.

23. Reynold A. Nicholson, *The Mystics of Islam* (London: Routledge and Kegan Paul, 1914), 125.

24. Subhan, *Sufism: Its Saints and Shrines*, 40.

3

PRACTICES OF FOLK MUSLIMS

The remainder of this book will encompass all of folk Islam. Many of the illustrations cited will have relevance to Sufism, but some practices will not fit easily into any category. Thus, the term *folk Islam* is used here in its widest sense.

The folk Muslim is a practitioner. To him, nothing can be so barren as cognitive religion. Existence takes on meaning as it is experienced on the stage of life where the actors are permitted the freedom to improvise their contribution to the drama of humanness. Little does it matter if he is misunderstood or maligned. Actually, he is convinced that it is the world—not himself—that is out of synchronization with life.

Over the years, I have traveled by train to and from outstations where I have been engaged in evangelistic outreach. I return to my home on the 9 P.M. train. My greatest relaxation on the trip, after a hot day in our center (which has no fan), has been to snuggle into a comfortable position on the second-class carriage bench, purchase seven cents worth of peanuts, and watch the "mystic of the day" perform. These "minstrels of the rails" move from carriage to carriage playing mystical songs on a one-string banjo and singing at the top of their voice. The lyrics speak of the "bird in the cage" or the "Beloved standing at the door of the tavern." There is something exotic about shelling peanuts, listening to the clickety-clack of the train wheels, and watching a mystic sing his heart out about a man in pursuit of God.

This chapter, then, will illustrate practices of the mystic community throughout the world. Much of what is documented will seem to be heretical. Some practices will be repugnant to the sensitive reader. But I would ask for more than a casual perusal of these next pages. It is necessary to look beyond form and investigate longings and unfulfilled needs. Can we identify, within this surging restlessness, a multitude of hungry hearts reaching out for a reality that can be more than adequately filled through a personal relationship with Christ? It is our responsibility to seek to answer this question.

ANIMISM

A special ritual, presided over by one or more imams, involves the Maulid-like recitation of the life-story of Prophet Muhammed and hymns in his praise, and also the weighing of the baby on an improvised scale balanced by a chicken, coconut, seedlings, and other ritual goods. At a certain point in the ceremony, the senior imam moistens the baby's hair with perfume and cuts off at least three locks of the hair. Sugar is then placed in the infant's mouth in the belief that thus as an adult he will utter sweet words. The severed locks of hair are inserted into a young coconut in which holes have been cut—and the coconut is later suspended on a nearby tree, marking the end of the ceremony.[1]

Animistic practices are almost always a remnant from the days before Muslims came to a people and converted them. One would think Islam would have purged such heretical influences from the lives of the new believers. Such is not the case. More often than not, the initial Muslim missionaries were Sufis or at least mystically influenced. They were in favor of accommodation and compromise rather than strictly holding to the letter of Islamic law. This was appreciated by the converts. They could retain much of the old and simply add to it that which seemed good and helpful. Cultural and religious conflict was minimized.

The resulting expression of Islam mixed with animism is indeed painful to the visiting Saudi Arabian diplomat!

Islam was extremely accommodating when it came to the Philippines. For example, Filipino Muslims currently perform a rice-planting ritual intended to appease the rice spirits in order that a good harvest may be secured. A spirit house is built at the center of the field. Certain cleansing ceremonies are carried out at the four corners of the plot of land. It is important for a religious man trained in Islamic law to plant the first seeds as well as harvest the initial crop. Such a ritual can be traced back to pre-Islamic times.[2]

Another rite of ancient practice found among Filipino Muslims relates to the curing of sickness by calling on the spirits. The religious leader applies herbs or roots to the diseased area of the body. When asked how such a practice can be in harmony with the teaching of Islam, the practitioner replies that he "can do nothing without the help of God; if he succeeds, it is the will of God."[3]

Also, much superstition centers around graveyards. In the southern Philippines the final three days of the month-long fast are known as *rikor*. During the last afternoon the gravestones are cleaned, and that evening they are lighted with candles or torches. This ceremony is known as "souls of the dead." It is believed that the spirits of the departed will return during this time to visit with living friends and relatives. Therefore, it is important to show respect to the cemetery, which is the abode for the dead and the place to which the spirits return.[4]

All religions, down through the centuries, have considered that blood possesses great mystical value. Ceremonies of blood sacrifice usually center around offering animals but have been known to include offering children and even adults. In Islam, however, the focus is on animals, particularly at the time of *Baqr Eid,* a festival that celebrates the willingness of Abraham to sacrifice his son to God. Charles R. Marsh has observed such a ceremony in Chad.

> The priest took the knife and drew it across the animal's throat. Facing the East towards Mecca, he said, *"Bismillah"* [in the name of God]. The crimson blood gushed over the sand. Immediately there was a wild rush of people. They

dipped their fingers in the blood and smeared it on their bodies. Some rubbed pieces of paper on it, and hastened to carry it to sick people to daub on their bodies. Others rushed with the blood to the door of their homes and smeared it on the lintel.[5]

I was able to confirm that this practice is regularly carried out in contemporary times in one Asian country I visited. Particularly valuable is the cloth that is placed under the cow's neck. The owner of the sacrificed animal has the privilege of attaching this bloodsoaked cloth to the lintel of his front door. This is said to bestow blessing on all who visit this man's home. It is interesting to speculate whether this practice has its roots in the Old Testament account of God's deliverance of the children of Israel from Egypt.

Another ceremony that takes place among the Muslims of Chad relates to fertility rites. The Baguirmi, a tribe that is wholly Muslim, send a regular contribution to the pagan priests of Abu Touyour, a mountain peak in the central region of Chad. The mountains of the area are designated either male or female. There are innumerable altars and "high places" in the region. Women desiring to bear children send significant offerings to the priests. Also, in times of drought, Muslims travel to the mountaintops and offer sacrifices for the purpose of persuading God to send rain.

There are humble folk-devotions, relics of a dim past of animistic belief in sacred stones, "high places," and haunting spirits. Such devotions, obscure, ignorant, and often full of faith, may play their part when an Egyptian peasant woman vows oil or lentils to the inhabitant of a whitewashed tomb among the mudbrick houses, or when an Arab village sacrifices a sheep to the wali of the neighboring hilltop.[6]

The practice of animism extends to the use of the Quran. Certain suras (chapters) are quoted in the belief that such a recitation of holy words will assist the devotee in obtaining good health.

Sura 113 is believed to be a deterrent to all sorts of disease.

Sura 114 has the power to counteract psychic afflictions.

Suras 94 and 105 are to be recited early in the morning as a safeguard against toothaches.

Sura 72 is to be quoted when one is fearful of the power of evil jinn.

Sura 13 is a cure for headaches.

Many Muslims, when ill, follow a ritual that seems baseless to the scientific-minded Westerner. A verse from the Quran will be written in ink or sandalwood paste on a plate or on the inside of a basin. The container will then be filled with water, which dissolves the writing. The water is poured into a glass and given to the patient to drink. Another method is to write the words of the Quran on a piece of paper and wash them off into a glass of water. Or, even more simply, an imam recites from the Quran and then breathes over a container of water. This then is given to the sick person to drink.[7]

A similar illustration comes from North Africa:

> At the mosque in Mammam the boys learn the Quran from wooden slates which are coated with whiting or chalk. The chapter of the Quran which is to be memorized is copied onto the slate with a pen made from a split reed. This is dipped in ink made from charred sheep's wool and gum. The water used to wash the slates clean is called the "Holy Water" and is kept in a large earthen jar outside the mosque. It is reputed to be a certain remedy for many complaints. The patients drink it, and this, of course, is equivalent to drinking the word of God.[8]

In the subcontinent a ceremony called *istikhara* is usually performed on Thursday nights, the favorite meeting time for Sufis. Six suras are recited from the Quran. Then the petitioner writes out his request on a piece of paper. This writing is fumigated with incense, bound with a piece of white thread, and placed in an earthenware pot full of water. The loose end of the thread is tied to the ear of the supplicant. He then lies down to sleep with his face toward Mecca. It is believed that the devotee will receive the answer to his prayer in a dream during the night.

The word *animism* has an extremely negative connotation to Jews, Christians, and Muslims. It is a word that refers to a corruption of general revelation rather than a specific unfolding of truth revealed to a chosen people. Animism indicates a system of understanding that developed along naturalistic lines. Man saw that rain was necessary for the growth of his crops, so he began to seek to influence the rain god in times of drought. Barren women, facing the ostracism of society, commenced to conceive of a fertility god that could relieve them of the stigma of being less than whole. The sun was perceived to be the greatest power in the universe; therefore it was natural to suppose that a god existed within that awesome ball of fire.

Muslims who are influenced by animism syncretize a very basic and inadequate knowledge of Islam with a fear and worship of the unseen spiritual and naturalistic forces of the cosmos. They are seeking to respond to felt needs. To the best of their simple understanding they are trying to interact with the power that they perceive to be resident in the universe.

DHIKR

Not all *dhikr* is performed in the same manner. An interesting insight into the mechanics of *dhikr* as practiced by one group is given by Muhammad Enamul Haq.

> The method by which the formula *"la ilaha illallah"* is used is as follows: holding the breath in the stomach, the syllable *"la"* should be drawn up along with the drawing of breath, till it reaches the back side of the head in accompaniment with its [the head's] leftward movement, and then in the protracted state of breath, the word "Allah" should be uttered with energy just at the moment the head, in course of its leftward turning, reaches the right shoulder; after this the words *"illallah"* should be pronounced in a protracted

condition of breath in such a way that the breath may reach its last destination *"Qalb"* when the protracted breath should be let out with great energy.[9]

There is great significance in the continual repetition of the word *Allah*. The tongue should linger at the palate of the mouth as A-lllll-aaaa-h is pronounced. During this time all extraneous thoughts are to be banished from the mind. However, it is permissible and even good to concentrate upon one's *pir* during *dhikr*. For variety, the pace can be quickened and the name *Allah* repeated in harmony with the heartbeat. This is a method of actually bringing Allah into one's very being. It is easy to discern the mystical element in this performance. The repetition is to be continued until the mind is completely submerged within the divine radiance of almighty God.

> Breath is of God. If God is manifest in anything, it is in breath. The activity of our physical being depends on our breath. This keeps up the rhythm of the pulse and the rhythm of the beats of the brain. The centers are kept up by the rhythm. If the rhythm stops, the centers stop. As the tick of the watch, so is the swing of the breath.[10]

Action is regarded as a psychological process. It creates pictures in the atoms of the body. In prayer, every atom of the body becomes activated. Even the blood cells perform in a concert of praise to God. Recently, I was talking to an educated government officer. He was attempting to explain to me the mystical unity that exists in all of God's creation through the presence of atoms. In his thinking, I was one with a table or a chair. I asked him if there would be chairs in heaven. He answered emphatically in the affirmative, but went on to explain that there will be certain changes in the physical qualities of the atoms. Therefore, we may not recognize chairs as chairs in the next life. This type of thinking permeates Islamic mysticism and finds an outlet in the practice of *dhikr*. During this mystical performance the atoms are assisting the believer in his outpouring of worship and praise to God.

There are many variations of the *dhikr*. Many of these are simply superstitions that are quite unworthy of a monotheistic religion like

Islam. For instance, some Chishtis believe that if a man sits cross-legged and pinches a vein called *kaimas* with his toes, then he is assured of a heart full of peace. This must be done during the performance of *dhikr* while saying, *"La-ilaha-il-lal-laho."*[11]

In northern Nigeria on Friday afternoons a group of devotees squats in a circle with a white "holy cloth" spread in the center. This cloth signifies the mystical presence of Muhammad. At about 5 P.M., at a sign from the leader, all begin to recite the first words of the Quran in a low voice that gradually becomes louder as the pace quickens. When the sun begins to set, these men recite the word *Allah* very slowly, gradually fading it out. In this group there is no striving for an experience of ecstasy. If a member of the group is unable to join the others, he is told to recite the *Tahil* ("There is no God but God") one thousand times and the word *Allah* five hundred times with the aid of a rosary.[12]

The Hadith are cited as authority for the importance of repeating the name of God. A devotee came to the Prophet and asked him, "What is the best and the most rewarded of all actions?" Muhammad replied, "The best of actions is this: to separate yourself from the world and to die while your tongue is moist with repeating the name of God."[13]

Some mystics follow eleven rules for *dhikr*:

1.   *Awareness of breathing.* The mind must be attuned to be secretly aware of everything, even the process of breathing. The brain should pulsate with perception of the various attributes of the Beloved. This increased awareness is an aid to achieving mystical union with God.

2.   *Travel in one's own land.* In a literal sense this applies to one's everyday actions. In a figurative sense the mystic is a traveler on a journey. In a sense, he is a pilgrim moving through a hostile world with his mind totally fixed on God.

3.   *Watching the feet.* When walking, the seeker must continually fix his gaze on his steps. I have watched in amazement as a group of ten men walked along a path in a straight line, each person looking straight down at his feet. The leader was calling out instructions that the other nine men immediately followed in uncanny unison. The mystical

meaning of such actions is that each person must be aware of where he is going in a metaphorical sense.

4. *Solitude in company.* The mind is to be totally concentrated so that even in the midst of other people the devotee can keep his thoughts directed toward God. No distraction should be allowed to pull him away from his Beloved. Most Muslims do their set prayer ritual with eyes open. I have often wondered if they are any more successful in combating mind wandering during prayer than is the average Christian who prays with his eyes closed.

5. *Remembering.* The mystic should constantly keep in mind his status as a dedicated seeker of God. In times of temptation he must remind himself that he is a holy person who is fleeing the distractions of the world. This almost automatic reaction will be effective in keeping him undefiled and separate from a hostile community of ungodly persons.

6. *Restraint.* The devotee must be a person of discipline. He should be able to restrain and control himself in a manner appropriate to the circumstances.

7. *General awareness.* The mystic is in the world though not of the world. In *dhikr* he is both present and absent. In a mystical sense he is in the spirit, yet he is aware of what is going on around him.

8. *Recollection.* Concentration brings about a process of recall in which all the attributes of God are reviewed.

9. *Pause of time.* During pauses in thinking, the devotee must recapitulate his actions and examine them. If his past deeds are unworthy, then he must repent and determine to do better in the future.

10. *Pause of numbers.* This refers to an awareness that the required number of repetitions of various phrases has been completed during *dhikr.*

11. *Pause of the heart.* During this pause the mind is trained to visualize the seeker's heart bearing the name of Allah.[14]

The Islamic mystic, Abu Said, writing in the tenth century, gave this testimony of involvement with *dhikr:*

I abandoned my studies and came home to Mayhana and retired into the niche of the chapel in my own house. There I sat for seven years, saying continually, "Allah! Allah! Allah!" Whenever drowsiness or inattention arising from the weakness of the human nature came over me, a soldier with a fiery spear—the most terrible and alarming figure that can possibly be imagined—appeared in front of the niche and shouted at me, saying, "O Abu Said, say Allah!" The dread of that apparition used to keep me burning and trembling for whole days and nights, so that I did not again fall asleep or become inattentive; and at last every atom in me began to cry aloud, "Allah! Allah! Allah!"[15]

Imad-ud Din, an Indian Muslim convert, adds his comments concerning his preconversion activities:

I wrote the name of God on paper 125,000 times. I cut out each word separately with scissors and wrapped them up each in a little ball of flour, and fed the fish of the river with them. My days were spent in this manner. During half of the night I slept and in the remaining half I sat up and wrote the name of God mentally on my heart.[16]

It is important to grasp the utter sincerity with which these men pursued a relationship with God. Their desire was to somehow receive more of God. How does the finite grasp the infinite? Man is so temporal, so sinful, so very far from God. The Muslim supplicant raises empty hands toward heaven when he prays. It is a gesture of humility. What can defiled man offer a holy and righteous God? One can only, through symbol and deed, cry out to the Lord for mercy and forgiveness. These two Muslims were only responding in the best manner possible according to their religious and cultural conditioning.

Meditation is the focal point of *dhikr*. The object of concentrating upon God is to elevate the soul. Meditation involves opening one's senses and faculties in a process that allows God to come in and fill the heart of the seeker. Through this process touch becomes more acute, sight becomes keener, as do the senses of hearing, taste, and smell. I well remember visiting a Hindu temple in Chicago. Seated in a back room, a beautiful young girl from a wealthy family was sharing her experience with a group of us from Trinity Evangelical Divinity School. We had gone to the temple to share Christ, but this Hindu devotee soon had turned the tables on us. She, with great sincerity, related what her *guru* meant to her. As she meditated very deeply on her *guru* as well as the multiplicity of Hindu gods, she came into a "final-stage" relationship with the infinite. At that point a sweet nectar was released from the brain and came into her mouth. When this happened, she was translated into a state of ecstasy. She had now reached a point of assimilation with god.

This girl went on to tell us of how she had been completely given over to drugs and promiscuity. Her parents had despaired of her. Now she had given up all sinful worldly activities. Meditation was to her the path of release and fulfillment. The enhancement of the sense of taste gave her assurance of having reached a stage of special relationship with the infinite presence. Folk Muslims often relate similar experiences.

Dhikrs are channels through which miracles are performed. Idries Shah has overviewed this process:

> *Dhikrs* are generally said during the hours of darkness. When a supernatural result is desired, the *dhikr* must dwell upon some facet of the Divine power allied to the effect to be accomplished. Thus, when a Sufi wishes to cure illness, he prepares himself by repeating a *dhikr* consisting of the Name of God which denotes healing. By this means the Sufi intends to collect in his mind a tremendous potential of mental force associated with healing. This he projects towards the object of his attentions, at the same time concentrating upon the desired result.

> When a Sufi's aid is invoked to ensure, for example, success in any venture, he will purify himself and spend three nights, culminating on a Thursday reciting the simple formula *Ya Fatih* (O Victor)—one of the attributes of the All-Powerful. On Thursday (the "powerful" night of the week) the full quota of power will have been built up on his mind: this,

at any event, is the theory. He may also give the person a talisman or amulet with a *dhikr* written on it to wear on his arm. Even today, these *dhikr* amulets are widely worn among all classes in the Muslim East. It is not uncommon for Sufis to receive a visitation from some important member of the Order—perhaps long dead—advising them as to the best course to take in any matter upon which they are uncertain.[17]

Certain types of folk Muslims deal quite extensively in the occult. They, through *dhikr,* claim the ability to relieve pain and cure disease. They are able, supposedly, to transport people anywhere in the world in the twinkling of an eye. They are able to foretell events as well as know what a person is thinking even though he is not present.

Dhikr, then, is a practice with many forms and purposes. It is a ceremony that is followed by both the sincere and the false. *Dhikr* can be used as a vehicle to come to know God or it can be exploited as an instrument of power to hurt or destroy. Such is the multifaceted expression of a religious practice loved and, in some instances, feared by millions of Muslims worldwide.

MYSTICAL LEADERSHIP

Charisma is a commonly accepted quality of leadership. For example, Billy Graham relates effectively to millions of people of disparate backgrounds. John F. Kennedy, in a short three years, had America and Americans at his feet. Mahatma Gandhi, a small, shriveled Hindu, was almost worshiped by a half billion Indians. What is charisma? Is it physical attractiveness, wealth, force of personality, or some mysterious mix of all three? It is very difficult to understand the components of charisma. A personable, handsome Christian with a doctoral degree can preach the exact sermon that Billy Graham does and leave his audience totally unmoved. Charisma is a quality that transcends religion, nationality, or ethnic identity.

In orthodox Islam there is little scope for a style of leadership that exalts a particular person. Each mosque has its own priest who ministers usually to a small group of worshipers. There is not an exact counterpart in Islam to the Christian denomination with its institutionalized hierarchy of leadership. In the political realm, however, there are leaders who have mobilized the masses by an appeal to the teachings of Islam.

Within folk Islam, on the other hand, men of great charisma have acquired followings that resemble those of leaders of cults. The next section will illustrate the practices of these men of great charisma.

PIRS

The saints of popular Islam are liberated men. They are regarded as having progressed beyond the confines of legalism.

> Many *pirs*, however, regard the law as a curb that is indeed necessary so long as one remains in the disciplinary stage, but may be discarded by the saint. Such a person, they declare, stands on a higher plane than ordinary men, and is not to be condemned for actions which outwardly seem irreligious. While the older Sufis insist that a *pir* who breaks the law is thereby shown to be an imposter, the popular belief in the saints and the rapid growth of saint-worship tended to aggrandise the *pir* at the expense of the law, and to foster the conviction that a divinely gifted man can do no wrong, or at least that his actions must not be judged by appearances.[18]

Who is a real *pir?* Recently, I was talking to a Muslim who is the general manager of a sugar factory that employs more than 1,700 persons. He was decrying the presence of the many *pirs* he regards as false. I took advantage of the opportunity to ask this educated mystic what qualities should be found in a true *pir.* He thought for a few moments and then replied, "First, the *pir* must keep all the laws of Islam. Secondly, he will not be a person concerned with financial gain. He is a man of spiritual perception. This will be his focus in life. Lastly, the *pir* will be honest and upright in all his dealings with people."

One very important consideration was omitted by my friend. The *pir* is expected to possess almost magical powers. "It is the saint who can avert calamity, cure disease, procure children for the childless, bless the efforts of the hunter, and even improve the circumstances of the dead."[19] In my opinion, this ability to perform miracles and meet felt needs is the root of the charisma of most *pirs*.

> The miracles that are attributed to Indian saints and *darvishes* are too numerous to enumerate. They include, for instance, walking on water, flying in the air (with or without a passenger), rain-making, appearing in various places at the same time, healing by the breath, bringing the dead to life, knowledge and prediction of future events, thought reading, turning earth into gold or precious stones, producing food and drink, etc. Besides these, thaumaturgic [(to perform miracles)] treatment of incurable and complicated diseases is one of the most characteristic miracles. Herbs, water, amulets, and the outward application or inward administration of many other insignificant things, the property of which is quite unknown to medical science, are the means of their thaumaturgic treatment.[20]

Pirs frequently claim power to transcend time and space. They reportedly have been seen at the same time in places many thousands of miles apart. Shayk Abdul-Qadir Julani, one of the most celebrated saints of Sufism, is believed to have traveled thousands of miles in an instant in order to be present at the funeral of a friend.[21] Flying enormous distances in full view of people on the ground is believed to be a common occurrence.

Sheikh Shahab-el-Din was able, it is said, to induce the presence of fruits, people, and objects at will. The story is related that he once requested the sultan of Egypt to place his head in a large bowl of water. Instantly, the sultan found himself transformed into a shipwrecked mariner cast ashore in an unknown land. He was rescued by woodcutters and brought to a nearby town where he commenced work as a slave. After a number of years, he gained his freedom, started a business, married, and settled down. His business eventually failed, and once again he undertook menial tasks in order to support his wife and seven children. One day he was down by the sea and decided to go for a swim.

Upon entering into the water, he immediately found himself back in the palace at Cairo. Once again he was a king surrounded by servants. The grave-faced sheikh was sitting in front of him. This total experience, although it had seemed to last for years, was said to have taken place in just a few seconds.[22]

Other activities of so-called saints can be questioned.

A blind *pir* was once asked to exorcise a jinn from a young man. He directed him to be seated on a mat and himself began to recite verses from the Quran, at the same time preparing some small rolls of cotton wool. When the recitation was over he sat for some time in deep meditation. Finally he called on his assistants to set alight the wool and let the smoke enter the youth's nostrils. Naturally there followed a fit of coughing and sneezing. The *pir* shouted, "Get out, you evil spirit, and leave him alone!" The youth looked dazed, so the *pir* repeated, "Are you going to clear out or must I use more severe measures?" In reply the young man muttered something inaudibly. So the *pir* ordered his assistants to beat the boy on the head with their shoes. While this was going on the patient cried and writhed with pain, the *pir* all the while repeating his question. At last the young man became unconscious. The beating was stopped, and the *pir* assured the parents that the evil spirit had departed and that they could take their son home. The boy died a week later, nor did the *pir* long survive him. A few months later he himself died in that same village and his grave is now a shrine for his disciples.[23]

The *pir* receives very special attention when he visits his disciples. Women minister to their *pir* much as they would to their own husbands. They wash his back, massage his legs, and serve him the best food they can afford. This is regarded as holy work and therefore evokes no jealousy in the husband.

A British friend of mine went to visit an acquaintance recently. As my friend is a foreigner, he received special treatment from this mystical Muslim. First, he washed my friend's feet, saying he had read in the Gospels about this exercise of humility on the part of Jesus Christ. Next, he applied cold cream to my friend's face and thoroughly rubbed it in. He then requested that my friend pray at the grave of his father. At the time of departure, the mystic gave my friend money equivalent to twenty-five cents. The significance of these activities will forever remain locked in the brain of this folk Muslim. Actually, the mystic doesn't desire to be rational. The less conformed he is to social norms, the greater is the proof of his mystical authenticity.

Recently, in a village, I met with a rather poor *pir* who has to work in a cloth factory in order to support his family of three wives and two boys. His following is small, but significant. He assured me he practices birth control with no aids other than mental concentration. Also, he is able to predetermine the sex of each of his children. Therefore, he has had a boy by each of his first two wives. He assured me his third wife would soon present him with a third boy.

Pirs are great storytellers. Each point in their sermons is reinforced by a relevant story from the culture and society of the listeners.

> The *pirs* never argue. No proof of their assertions are ever advanced. But they give you wonderful illustrations and beautiful stories. Their words come straight from the heart. On the relationship of God and man, for instance, they would say: The hearts of men are like the boats on the ocean that is God; He moves them as He likes; He carries them with the rising tide and leaves them on the desert land, where they must wait till once more He comes and takes them to a beautiful island. On the question whether it is right for a Hindu to go to a Muslim saint or vice versa, they would ask, "Does the butterfly that loves the light inquire about the caste and the religion of the person in whose house it finds it?"[24]

This illustration highlights a rather refreshing and at the same time disturbing belief propagated among mystics. Firstly, the positive feature of such broad-mindedness and acceptance is, in contrast to the more orthodox Muslim, an almost total lack of attacking adherents of other religions. Folk Muslims are syncretistic and do not follow only one path in their quest for God. A good mystic would rejoice to hear of a friend who has found God—regardless of the path utlilized in his pursuit. In this vital area, he is much like the Hindu who repeatedly asserts that all roads lead to God.

On the other hand, it is difficult to witness for the Christian faith to a group that does not make necessary distinctions among the great variety of religious beliefs and practices prevalent in the world today. However, the mystic does stress the necessity of a personal encounter with God. This important belief will be further explored in chapter 5.

URS

The word *urs* means "marriage." The followers of a *pir* believe that in death there will be a marriage or union between their guide and God. Hence, the anniversary of the *pirs'* death is celebrated with singing, dancing, *dhikr*, and sermonizing. There is a widespread belief that the *pir* in heaven will be extremely displeased unless the anniversary is celebrated with great festivity on the part of the disciples. "Cows, goats, and fowls are generally slaughtered on this occasion in the name of the *pir*. The meat is served as a feast to those who attend the ceremony. On this occasion a fair is held which lasts from a day up to a month."[25]

> Devotees of the saints attending the celebrations are believed to acquire merit. It would be an endless task to attempt to describe the particular rites attached to the *urs* of individual saints, but the form the worship generally takes on the occasion of such visits combine such features as these: Suras 1; 112; 113; and 114 are recited; these are followed by the repetition of certain prayers for the soul of the departed; finally, the worshiper makes some personal requests. As a rule, a vow is made at this time which must be paid at the tomb when the favor is granted. It is a common practice to tie bits of thread or pieces of cloth etc. in gratings near the tomb, by way of reminding the saint of the favor asked.[26]

The Prophet was said to have given warning against making tombs a place of worship. Still, such veneration started very early among Muslims. This may have been due to the influence of then-prevalent

Christian saint worship in Syria and Egypt. The practice soon spread into Iran, where today more than a thousand known and unknown persons are worshiped.[27]

There is a great difference between worship in a mosque and a shrine. The congregational prayer time in the mosque is a time of dignity and order. Ritual is an essential part of the ceremony. There is no singing or idle talking. God is the focus of attention. In contrast, the *urs* provides an opportunity for men, women, and children to give way to their inner feelings of devotion for a man they believe was a special saint of God. Although he is dead and buried, yet the devotees believe in his continuing ability to hear their prayers and intercede on their behalf before God. In the shrine (or royal court, as some call it) the disciples are free to honor their *pir* in whatever manner they choose. I have even heard of extreme instances in one country where devotees work into such a frenzy of emotion that they throw off their clothes and dance in the nude with hands uplifted toward God. This is, of course, not the norm, but it is an illustration of disciples going into a state of ecstasy in which abnormal behavior takes place.

The following examples describe saint worship as it takes place in many countries around the world:

I received a letter from a missionary friend in Pakistan who updates the happenings at the tomb of Babu Farid, whom I mentioned in chapter 1. "During the last few days the *urs* of Babu Farid Ganj-i-Shaker has been held at Pak Paltan. An item in the newspaper yesterday said that during the last twenty-four hours over fifty thousand pilgrims passed through the 'Bahishti Darwaza' [Door to Paradise]." Walking through this door is supposed to assure the devotee of entrance into heaven.

Another instance from the Punjab of Pakistan illustrates the influence of poetry within Sufi ranks.

The Punjab is unrivalled for the number of its Sufi shrines. Every few miles there are one or two of them. There is hardly a shrine which does not possess some traditional verse of its own. The *Kavvalis* there sing of the saints and their poetry.

Credulous admirers still gather there in large numbers, to admire and worship the saints who, singing of the Beloved, were ultimately merged in Him. The Punjabis still consider themselves fortunate to have such noble, pious, and sweet poetry which inspires them to seek the Divine Love.[28]

In Malaysia, the Muslim is seen frequently at the grave of some renowned saint. His main purpose for going there is to make a petition to God through the departed *pir*. A piece of cloth is tied to a nearby tree to remind the spirit of the petition. Other devotees at the shrine will write a verse of the Quran on a slip of paper and swallow it. This will, they believe, ensure good health.

A reporter recently visited the interior of Russia and found thousands of Muslims going annually to the Al Bukhari mausoleum and the Sumbul *mazar*. The local newspaper, *Bakinski Rabochi*, criticized "fanatical" Muslims for practicing self-flagellation during their religious pilgrimages.

An advertisement in a large-circulation English daily newspaper in Bangladesh told of the 676th *urs* anniversary of Hazrat Nizamuddin Aulia to be held in New Delhi. The item stated, "Special prayers will be arranged on this auspicious occasion. All the desires of your anguished heart and soul for worldly and spiritual attainments can *Inshallah* be fulfilled by attending this holy *urs* celebration."

Many activities take place at the *urs*. Some of these illustrations I have researched from reputable sources. Other descriptions are of events which I have personally observed.

> A woman petitioner at a *mazar* sat on a low stool before the *pir* and told of her desire to have a child. She was asked if she had brought with her the seeds and milk as specified. The milk was produced in a small metal teapot, the seeds wrapped up in paper. The *pir* thereupon took the seeds, scattered them upon the milk, breathed over it, and carefully replacing the lid instructed the woman how and when to drink it. Most of the time his lips moved quietly as though he were repeating some verses. He then bound two of the pieces of paper,

containing Quran verses, in two tiny rolls of cloth and told the woman to wear one around her neck and the other at her waist. The woman was finally told to go home and live in the power of those charms to give her the desire of her heart. She went away expressing her sincere gratitude and promising that her small gifts would be followed by something more generous.[29]

A very close Muslim friend and I left a district town around 11 A.M. in a dilapidated bus for a ten-mile journey to the shrine of a well-known *pir*. Arriving in a small market center, we left the bus and quickly negotiated a price of one dollar for a four-mile backbreaking journey by horsecart to the site of the *mazar* where a special meeting is held each Friday at 1 P.M. While bouncing along on the rutted dirt road, we saw scores of people making their way to the shrine. Everyone seemed friendly and in a festive mood.

Upon arrival, we were confronted with a large crowd of hundreds of people. The focus of attention seemed to be on huge baskets and pans in which people were dumping their offerings of specially prepared rice and meat curry. The food was of high quality. Children by the scores were running about, many trying to divert the attention of the attendants while a conniving friend would steal a bit of chicken from the pot. Over to one side was a table behind which several men were sitting recording in huge notebooks the cash and kind gifts of the devotees. They were also selling the chickens, eggs, and sweets, and putting the profits with the other money. The offerings were to pay pledges that devotees had made to the departed *pir*. These people were firm believers in his continuing power. Therefore, they prayed to him saying if he would grant them certain petitions, they would give gifts at his *mazar*. From the look of the mounds of food, the devotees were having a lot of prayers answered!

Just at 1 P.M. the men made their way over to the mosque where they participated in the age-old ritual of saying prayers in Arabic as orthodox Muslims do the world over. Following prayers, bedlam broke loose as the food was distributed to all present. Anyone, man, woman, or child, who felt slighted as to the quantity received let it be known in the loudest possible voice. The children enjoyed getting a share at one distribution point, quickly consuming it, and rushing to a different dispenser. They then assumed a look of one suffering from acute malnutrition, meanwhile pressing an empty bowl toward the dispenser's basket full of rice.

My friend and I walked over to the *mazar,* which was a short distance from the mosque. We removed our shoes before we entered the courtyard. The old tomb was inside a recently built shelter. Flowers were spread all around the area. The heavy smell of burning incense permeated the air. No one knew the name of the *pir,* much less his claims, legitimate or otherwise, to such fame being accorded him. We heard all kinds of estimates as to the year he died. But the important thing is the firm belief that his power is resident at the *mazar* and in the lives of his devotees. My friend, an orthodox Muslim, was told to face the *mazar* and pray for whatever he needed. He considered such a suggestion blasphemous—and proceeded in front of everyone to say his prayers toward Mecca in the prescribed fashion. As a concession to local sentiments, we walked out of the tomb area backward so that we would show no disrespect to the *pir* by turning our backs to him. We were then invited to go and sit inside the mosque for a delicious meal of rice and curry. All the bearded Muslims who sat chatting with us were extremely gracious and friendly.

My friend and I decided to walk the four miles back to the main road rather than suffer the indignities pushed upon us by first-century transportation systems. As we walked through the lush countryside observing the beauties of God's wonderful creation, my friend reached over and took my hand (an Eastern sign of close friendship between two males) while he sought, with the other hand, to subdue the fierce struggles of the chicken that he had just purchased at a "bargain rate" at the *mazar.* Suddenly, in a beautiful voice, he began to sing some of the lyrics of past, great mystical poets. It was a fitting conclusion to a journey into a world of contrasts—contrasts of joy, sorrow, fear, hope, love, anxiety, and devotion.

In one Muslim country the "turtle pond" is a well-known religious center for pilgrimage. As my family and I drove up to the gate just off the main road, we were besieged by vendors who sought to sell us bread and raw meat that had been attached to the end of long thin sticks. This offering of food could be conveniently fed to the turtles. Other stalls sold garlands of flowers and boxes of incense which could be given as offerings at the grave of the *pir*.

The actual history of this *pir* is lost in antiquity. This, however, allows for the many apocryphal stories that are related by his devotees. Observing the huge plot of land and the large pond, we knew that the *pir* had done well financially. His disciples were said to have numbered in the thousands.

We walked over to the pond where we saw many turtles swimming about. They ranged in size from large sea turtles to babies. On one side of the pond were steps leading down into the water. A number of people were carefully plunging the raw meat on the end of their sticks into the open mouths of rather fierce-looking turtles. All were being very careful not to get their feet close to the hungry turtles.

Men, women, and children were milling about the area. Some of the women were wearing black, shapeless veils. Beggars accosted us with their usual vitality. In an effort to understand why people had come from great distances to feed these turtles, I interviewed several of the pilgrims. Their answers to my questions were enlightening.

A young student gave me a bit of historical insight on the *pir*. The saint had a great love for the turtles and thus brought them into this pond from the nearby sea. In his honor people come from all over the world to feed the turtles that had meant so much to the *pir*.

One boy was carefully filling a small bottle with the filthy, slimy pond water. He enthusiastically told me this water would be taken back to his home and kept for the purpose of anointing the sick. It was his belief that the water contained power to heal the diseased and infirm.

Another student was busily engaged in feeding a large number of turtles. He was pleased to tell me that this was his thank offering in response to having recently passed his exams.

A man declared that there was great spiritual power in the area around the pond. One could call upon the saint in prayer to intercede in his behalf to God.

Yet another person spoke of the spirits in the turtles which, when released, could be of great assistance to the petitioner.

Just a few yards from the turtle pond, incongruously, stands a traditional mosque representing a ritualistic Islam that is the antithesis of all the activity swirling around it. Yet the mosque is very much a part of the total scene. Many pilgrims were inside praying in response to the call to prayer that continues to go forth from the minaret five times a day.

Over to one side, we found a man busily accepting the shoes of the pilgrims. A small fee was paid for the assurance that one's shoes would be retrievable on one's return from a visit to the saint's shrine. Barefooted, we walked up the steep stairway to the top of a hill that afforded a stunning view of the pond area as well as the city and nearby sea. The tomb was very well-kept with a blooming flower garden at the entrance.

My seventeen-year-old daughter started to enter the veranda of the shrine. She was stopped by the "moneychangers" who were sitting at a table collecting gifts from the pilgrims who were leaving the building. She was told to go over to a side room where the women were restricted to a distant look at the tomb. Inside, I found many men praying toward the saint's *mazar*. The room was filled with the heavy smoke of incense. Pilgrims were taking slips of paper, writing out their petitions on them, and then leaving the rolled-up paper either on the tomb or along the side on a railing. Well-dressed men were lost in mystical contemplation as they stood near the remains of a saint who they are convinced lives on today in spirit and in power. After prayer, all slowly backed out of the room toward the men on the veranda who were eagerly awaiting their donations.

A little distance from the *mazar* we met a group of long-haired musicians. They were happy to perform a musical concert for a small fee. These men were the transient *faqirs* who are to be found on buses, trains, and in most public places. Although people do not approve of their *ganja*-smoking excesses, they thoroughly enjoy their mystical songs.

I came away from this experience simply amazed that Muslim fundamentalists do not protest such an animistic, syncretistic expression of Islam. As far as I know, there has never been such a protest on any significant scale.

A word needs to be said concerning the large number of women found at the *mazars*.

> It is a common sight to see numbers of women at these shrines, and unveiled at that. The explanation given is that the sanctity of the place is itself a protection against molestation by men. They are permitted to come to make their requests and perform their vows, but at certain tombs they are strictly forbidden from entering the enclosure of the shrine proper.

> Curious reasons are sometimes given for such exclusion. For instance, women are not allowed to enter the shrine of Dadi-u-din at Makanpur, Cawnpore (d. A.D. 1485), because it is believed that any woman doing so will be seized immediately with violent pains, "as if her whole body were wrapped in flames of fire." Outside the shrine of Miyan Mir, Lahore (d. A.D. 1635), there hangs a notice in Urdu and English forbidding entrance to women. Nor is it only from the shrines of well-known saints that women are excluded. At a small tomb in Delhi women are not allowed past the railing because the saint is reputed to have the power of looking through a woman, even though she is fully clothed.[30]

Women may be considered second-class citizens at the *mazars* but still they are among the most enthusiastic supporters of the *urs*. One of the main reasons relates to the issue of fertility.

> Many women who visit these shrines hope thereby to give birth to a son. Thus a childless Pathan woman will often journey many a weary mile to some shrine and there hang up

a rag torn from her clothing in the belief that the reproach of barrenness will thus be removed.

Frequently there is to be seen planted at the head of a tomb a godini tree, which bears little red berries. A sterile woman will be given some of these to eat after some Quranic passage has been recited over them, and she will make a vow to give something to the saint when her desire is fulfilled.[31]

In some *mazars* the bricklayers make a hole in the wall near the tomb. On Thursday nights women will place food in this crevice. Women of poorer classes perform this rite in the belief that angels come in the night and eat the food placed there. The angels are therefore pleased with the behavior of the supplicant and will assist her by interceding with God on her behalf.

FINANCES

Perhaps the whole system of folk Islam is most vulnerable at the point of finances. For example, many of the minstrels are regarded as social dropouts and financial parasites. I have seen travelers on trains get extremely irritated when a mystical singer has completed his "concert" and then makes a plea for gifts. Often he is encouraged, in rude language, to give up his itinerancy and settle down to a steady, legitimate job. The plea falls on deaf ears. To the mystic, his singing is more than a way to earn a living; it is a whole way of life. His being is totally wrapped up in encountering God. Song and verse are only externalized expressions of who he is.

Many, if not most, *pirs* are considered to be more interested in money and power than souls. To the vast majority of disciples, this is not even an issue. They are happy to support the *pir* in return for some tangible assistance that meets their needs. But the unbeliever looks on from afar and scoffs at what he perceives as nothing more than a successful business enterprise. There is a parallel here with how some Christians view Rex Humbard, Oral Roberts, and the late Kathryn Kuhlman. The critics are external to the inner circle of disciples. Devotees care little for the ethics or otherwise of numerous mansions, fifty-thousand-dollar cars, and private jets. They are seeing in their teacher a representative of God who possesses spiritual power and who can lead them on to know the Lord.

It must be said that few *pirs* can begin to compare financially with wealthy Christian leaders in the West. Yet, on a local level, they often create jealousy and malice by having so much more materially than their counterparts within orthodox Islam. The advertisement that follows appeared in a newspaper in one Muslim country.

> If you are unable to attend the *urs,* you may take part in the *fateha* of *urs sharif* by sending your money for purposes of the *Nazar-o-Niyaz* by money order to my following office under intimation to me. By letter in this way, you may seek even being at home the pleasures and blessings of Hozrat Khwaja Sahib. Your money will be spent on sacred purposes as per your wish. Prayer will be offered at the holy tomb in your favor. The sacred *Tabbarukat* of the *urs fateha* will be sent to you after the *urs sharif* by post.[32]

The *tabbarukat* is a communication from the *pir* to the donor. A Muslim friend of mine received a letter from an acquaintance in Damascus. Upon opening the letter he found a small piece of cloth. This cloth was part of the huge covering that had been placed over the tomb of a famous *pir.* The attendants received offerings from devotees and then gave each donor a small piece of the holy cloth, which had become empowered by contact with the tomb. My friend was very pleased to receive such a gift of deep religious meaning.

Attendants at the *mazars* receive a percentage of all gifts given in memory of the *pirs*. My research indicates that on the average about one-third of all offerings goes to those who are responsible for collections. The rest of the money is designated for upkeep and salaries of caretakers. In some places money is used to assist the poor through the provision of primary schools and small clinics. However, accountability for expenditures is minimal, if it exists at all.

I have seen a collector going around from house to house and shop to shop collecting subscriptions for an upcoming *urs*. His notebook indicated many gifts had been solicited and received.

The system is open to simple misappropriation of funds. In one meeting a saint promised to bestow great blessings on those who donated to his causes. He started with higher amounts and asked those who agreed to give to raise their hands. Slowly, he decreased his request to the point where even the poorest person present could afford to give. The manipulative techniques of that *pir* could teach even some of our cleverest Christian fundraisers in the West a new trick or two!

One *pir* with a small following in a remote village stipulates that each devotee must give him two dollars each year. This is the minimum. At the annual meeting it is expected that a family will give at least another two dollars. However, the pressure at the time of taking the offering is such that few can resist giving larger amounts.

All would agree that full-time religious workers must receive an income adequate to meet their needs. As is true in Christianity, the ones who take advantage of the system bring disrepute to all.

A CASE STUDY: THE BAULS

This short description of one mystical group has been researched empirically through my interaction with individuals as well as through visits to Baul meetings. The academic notes on the Bauls have been gleaned from *The Bauls of Bangladesh,* which is written by Anwarul Karim, noted folklorist and director of the Lalon Academy in Kushtia, Bangladesh.

The exact date of the origin of the Baul cult has been lost in antiquity. There are few references to the Bauls in medieval literature. Mention of this sect is made in Maladhar Basu's *Sree Krishna Vijoy,* which was written in the fourteenth century. Other subsequent references prove that the Bauls existed in the fourteenth and fifteenth centuries. These texts show the Baul movement came into being through Muslim mysticism. The actual derivation of the word *Baul* is unknown, although scholars speculate it may have come from words which in English mean "mod," "crazy," "devoted friend," or "impatiently eager." Today the Bauls are found throughout Bangladesh and in many parts of India.

The Bauls enjoy wide popularity because of their singing of mystical songs. Many people are dissatisfied with a materialistic orientation to life. They have felt attracted to this group of nonconformists who constantly, in speech and song, appeal for a deeper and more personal relationship with God.

> In the West people become hippies. They are fed up with the society they live in. The Persian Sufism of which the Bauls are also a part might have influenced them. Yet, hippies and the Bauls are poles apart. Hippies are of modern origin, but Bauls are not. They have a past as well as a glorious future. They are the mainspring of a whole range of literature, poetry, and music. Occasionally they are misunderstood. Some have abandoned wandering and have opted to settle down. In part of Kushtia District there are Baul villages. Many are quite rich. Some have made a fortune by selling *ganja* or participating in special radio and television shows. The Bauls have a magical knowledge about self, occult training, and the mystery of the body. They have constructed a shortcut by which people may come to attain knowledge of God.[33]

Many male Bauls do not marry but keep a woman in a type of common-law relationship. She is known as an associate rather than a wife. Most Bauls smoke *ganja*, a powerful drug that is sold openly in the subcontinent. They usually smoke *ganja* in clusters at the time of group singing. Baul men wear loose pants and shirts. Their hair grows long and flows down over their shoulders. Bauls do not use a comb or brush, so their straggly hair and beards give them a distinctive unconventional look. Often they will wear beads around their necks. They carry shoulder bags and walk with curved sticks in their hands. Bauls are generally vegetarians, but at certain festivals they will eat fish.

Bauls place high value on their mantra, the word of mystery that carries great spiritual significance for the individual. Each Baul has a guide to show him the path of light. It appears that Muhammad and Krishna are the ultimate guides in the process of spiritual attainment. Bauls hold the Prophet in high esteem and believe that within him is fully represented the power of God.

Man, to the Bauls, is very important. He is made in the image of God and therefore, regardless of caste or creed, should be honored. Both body and soul are important, but the body will perish after death, while the soul is indestructible.

Bauls teach that the more mystical aspects of their belief can be understood only by the initiated. Outsiders can enjoy the poems and songs but will never come to fully appreciate the truths of Baulism unless brought into the inner group. Baul songs are full of unconventional symbols, imagery, and riddles. Their most famous esoteric song states:

> How does the unknown bird move in and out of the cage?
> If I could catch the bird, I would put the fetter of my heart
>   around its feet.
> The cage has eight cells and nine doors, besides small
>   openings at points.
> And on the top of it is a mirror chamber.
> On my heart, the cage you pursue is made of raw bamboo.
> It may collapse any day.
> The bird will then open up the cage and escape.
> No one knows where he will go.

Lalon Shah, who lived in Kushtia, is the venerated *pir* of the Bauls. He lived in the last century and was widely recognized for his literary talents as well as his spiritual quest for God. His *mazar* is in the suburbs of Kushtia. I have visited his *urs* and seen the thousands of disciples who come to listen to the song-fest that goes on nonstop for three days and nights. Baul songs are often punctuated with the phrase *Lalon says*. Without doubt, Lalon was a great syncretizer of religions, as this song illustrates.

> Everyone asks what religion or birth does Lalon belong to?
> Lalon says, I have never experienced the exact nature of either
>   religion or birth.

> If one is circumcised he is a Muslim, but what is the rule for
> women?
> I recognize the Brahmin because of his sacred thread, but how
> do I recognize the female Brahmin?
> Some wear a string of beads around their neck. But does this
> change their birth or religion?
> What caste is announced by a person at his birth and death?
> Water, when it is found in a ditch, is called ditch water.
> When it is found in the river Ganges it is called Ganges water.
> But originally it is all the same water.
> The difference is only how it is kept.

Such simplistic doctrine has a Hindu basis. All paths are equal and all lead to God. One will go by this road while another takes a different but equally valid route. This makes Bauls easy to live with but rather hard to win to Christ.

So it is apparent that Bauls are reacting against what they consider to be an overemphasis on ritual on one hand and materialism on the other. They want to be free—free to fly away into the bosom of the Beloved and be at rest. This world deflects them from their desire to know God. What better thing than to have a foretaste of heaven through using drugs and filling one's bosom with the songs of the mystics.

There is a parallel here with the impact Hinduism has made on Western youth. The Krishna cult looks attractive to young people who are disgusted with a society that dictates success in terms of new cars, large houses, and beachfront cottages. They are in pursuit of a new reality—a reality they themselves cannot explain. However, they are willing to experiment as long as the options are outside the "establishment."

Bauls, as well as all Muslim mystics, are crying into the dark. They want light. Their hearts are hungry, but, unfortunately, even in their openness they have created a closed system. Their way is superior. Lalon is the *pir* of *pirs*. Islam, Hinduism, Buddhism, and Christianity are all components to truth, but inadequate in their institutionalized forms. Man is not made to be bound. He must be free.

But what is freedom? In my view, the Bauls have not yet satisfactorily given an answer to that question.

NOTES

1. Peter G. Gowing, *Muslim Filipinos—Heritage and Horizon* (Quezon City: New Day Publishers, 1979), 67.

2. Ibid., 65.

3. Inger Wulff, "Continuity and Change in a Yakan Village," *Dansalan Quarterly*, vol. 1, no. 3 (April 1980), 154.

4. Nagasura Madale, "Ramadhan as Observed in Lanao," *Mindinao Journal*, vol. 1, no. 3 (1975), 19.

5. Charles R. Marsh, *Streams in the Sahara* (Bath, England: Echoes of Service, 1972), 4.

6. Constance E. Padwick, *Muslim Devotions: A Study of Prayer-Manuals in Common Use* (London: S.P.C.K., 1961), 235.

7. Violet Rhoda Jones and L. Bevan Jones, *Woman in Islam* (Lucknow: Lucknow Publishing House, 1941), 365.

8. Charles R. Marsh, *Too Hard for God* (Bath, England: Echoes of Service, 1970), 67–68.

9. Muhammad Enamul Haq, *A History of Sufi-ism in Bengal* (Dacca: Asiatic Society of Bangladesh, 1975), 104.

10. Hazrat Inayat Khan, *The Sufi Message of Hazrat Inayat Khan* (London: Barrie and Rockliff, 1962), vol. 7, 142.

11. Thomas P. Hughes, *Notes on Muhammadanism*, 3d ed. (London: W. H. Allen, 1894), 248.

12. J. Spencer Trimingham, *Islam in West Africa* (Oxford: Clarendon, 1959), 100.

13. Titus Burckhardt, *An Introduction to Sufi Doctrine*, trans. D. M. Matheson (Lahore: Shaikh Muhammad Ashraf, 1959), 133.

14. Idries Shah, *Oriental Magic* (Tonbridge, England: Octagon Press, 1968), 75.

15. Reynold A. Nicholson, *Studies in Islamic Mysticism* (Cambridge: At the University Press, 1921), 8–9.

16. Samuel M. Zwemer, *Islam: A Challenge to Faith* (New York: Student Volunteer Movement for Foreign Missions, 1907), 146.

17. Shah, *Oriental Magic*, 69.

18. Reynold A. Nicholson, *The Mystics of Islam* (London: Routledge and Kegan Paul, 1914), 127.

19. Anwarul Karim, *The Bauls of Bangladesh* (Kushtia: Lalon Academy, 1980), 57.

20. Haq, *History of Sufi-ism in Bengal*, 110–111.

21. Shah, *Oriental Magic*, 62.

22. Ibid., 61–62.

23. Jones and Jones, *Woman in Islam*, 349–350.

24. Hira Lal Chapra, "Sufism," in *The Cultural Heritage of India*, ed. Haridas Bhattacharyya, vol. 4, *The Religions* (Calcutta: Ramakrishna Mission Institute of Culture, 1956), 607–608.

25. Haq, *History of Sufi-ism in Bengal*, 325.

26. John A. Subhan, *Sufism: Its Saints and Shrines* (Lucknow: Lucknow Publishing House, 1938), 107.

27. A. M. A. Shushtery, *Outlines of Islamic Culture*, vol. 1, *Historical and Cultural Aspects* (Bangalore: Bangalore Press, 1938), 230.

28. Lajwanti Rama Krishna, *Panjab Sufi Poets A.D. 1460–1900* (Karachi: Indus Publishers, 1977), 134.

29. Jones and Jones, *Woman in Islam*, 315.

30. Ibid., 311–312.

31. Ibid., 313–314.

32. Sahibzada Syed Riyasat Husain, "Urs Mubarak 1981 of Hazrat Khwaja Moinuddin Chishty (R. A.) Ajmir Sharif [India]," handbill advertising a meeting, 1981.

33. Karim, *The Bauls of Bangladesh*, 7.

4

A Critique of Folk Islam

It is important to note that not all folk Muslims are as extreme, emotional, or corrupted as some of those cited in chapter 3. There are *pirs* who sincerely seek to lead their disciples in the path of godliness. Recently, I attended a three-hour meeting that contained little that I could criticize. This *urs* was arranged by a very gracious and influential man in the town in which I resided.

The meeting commenced at 5 P.M. under a gaily decorated tent that had been specially erected to accommodate the expected crowd. Women went into the adjacent house of the sponsor of the *urs*. Men, all wearing prayer hats, sat cross-legged on the cloth floor of the tent. The middle-aged *pir* had arrived with six of his close associates. We were told that the *pir* was suffering from high blood pressure and would not be able to participate significantly in the meeting. One of the first events of the evening was beautiful chanting in a language most of the people attending could not understand. I was told the chants started with the exaltation of the prophets and then praised the most significant *pirs* of this particular *tarika*. The chants were emotional, and it was evident the people attending were deeply moved. In this case the medium was even more powerful than the message. It is true that all understood the chanting was of an intensely religious nature.

The first speaker of the evening was a polished orator. He gave a sermonette on the offering of Abraham's son. The emotional trauma of the cost of obedience was narrated with pungency. Soon several of the men were wiping tears from their eyes. Another speaker droned on for forty-five minutes, and just about succeeded in putting the audience to sleep. The last exhortation came from a man who said that, at Allah's command, he left his dying mother to come to the meeting. He urged all present to have a vital relationship with God, one that would lead on to high morals and involvement in the needs of others.

At last the *pir* took the microphone and spoke in a low voice for only ten minutes. He gave his lineage from his *tarika's* original *pir.* This was done to establish his authenticity. Lastly, protracted prayer was offered by the first speaker of the evening.

Every half hour during the meeting, scented water was sprinkled over the audience. Also, I noted that at the mention of Muhammad or any *pir* the men would put their hands over their faces and make a clicking sound with their tongues. This was done as a sign of respect for the departed religious leaders.

As the three hundred devotees filed out, many were given a box that contained delicious rice and curry. The rest of us were asked to sit in long rows and were then served in a special, individual manner. My wife and the other women had followed the service from behind the curtains of the nearby house. The women were fed separately from the men.

In retrospect, I would give this *urs* very high marks for dignity as well as content. It is true there was frequent reference to the prophets and their teaching. Also, other religious men were cited favorably. But is this not done in an average Christian meeting in the West? Paul and John, as well as D. L. Moody and Billy Graham, are mentioned as men who are authorities on religious issues. The people at this gathering were being exhorted constantly to love God and fervently follow his path. After the meeting, I questioned the polished orator as to his view of God's law. He gave an answer similar to that which a Christian would give. This was in contrast to some Sufis who flagrantly violate God's commands in order to prove their freedom from the law.

Thus, I would not fault these men for methodology or overall aims. They want to know God. Their path, at least what I observed, was one of dignity. But, as a Christian, I am forced to disagree with important areas of substance. They see Jesus Christ as only a prophet, not the Savior of mankind who was God incarnate; the Bible is only part of God's revelation and has less authority than the Quran; salvation is by faith and works, not by grace alone.

This chapter will critique folk Islam in general terms. It is impossible to be exhaustive in these few pages. However, the comments will be suggestive and may lead others to engage in a more thorough critique.

THE TEACHING OF UNIVERSALISM

Hazrat Inayat Khan presents a description of Sufism that causes us to realize the complex nature of the beliefs with which we are dealing.

Sufism cannot be called a religion because it is free from principles, distinctions and differences, the very basis on which religions are founded; neither can it be called a philosophy, because philosophy teaches the study of nature in its qualities and varieties, whereas Sufism teaches unity. Therefore, it may best be called simply the preparation of the view.

The word "Sufi" implies purity, and purity contains two qualities. Pure means unmixed with any other element, or in other words, that which exists in its own element, unalloyed and unstained. The second quality of purity is great adaptability.

Such is also the nature of the Sufi. In the first place he purifies himself by keeping the vision of God constantly before him, not allowing the stains of earthly differences and distinctions to be mirrored upon his heart, nor good or bad society, nor intercourse with high or low class people. Nor can a faith or a belief ever interfere with his purity.

The Sufi shows his universal brotherhood in his adaptibility. Among Christians he is a Christian, among Jews he is a Jew,

among Muslims he is a Muslim, among Hindus he is a Hindu:
for he is one with all, and thus all are one with him. He allows
everyone to join in his brotherhood, and in the same way
he allows himself to join in any other. He never questions,
"What is your creed or nation or religion?" Neither, does he
ask, "What are your teachings or principles?"

Call him brother, he answers brother, and he means it.[1]

The teaching of religious universalism is a doctrine of convenience.
It is inclusive rather than exclusive. Such a teaching leads to a high
degree of social acceptance. Sufis glory in their broad-mindedness. Islam
is their foundation; but it is quite permissible to adulterate religious forms
and expressions in order to accommodate diverse preferences. However,
we believe the Christian message cannot be just another way to God.
Scripture is unequivocal as to the uniqueness of salvation only through
the person and work of Jesus Christ.

Recently, I was talking to a mystic who has become a believer in
Christ. This man was expressing repugnance at some of the activities
he observed while he was an active participant in one of the *tarikas*.
He asked how followers of God could be sexually promiscuous, smoke
marijuana, and generally be a drag on society. The mystic would respond
that he was only doing that which, to him, is spiritually meaningful. Once
again, we find such behavior and lax attitudes toward biblical norms of
morality to be an area of serious disagreement between folk Muslims
and Christians.

Folk Muslims pay little attention to the study of holy books. Mystics
see such a study as diversionary. Therefore, there is little self-criticism
within folk Islam. Either one accepts the total message or leaves the fold.
This is true of orthodox Islam as well. I have never seen a book written
by a Muslim that questions the authority of the Quran. In this respect
Islam is indeed deviant from truth because of the lack of openness to
criticism from within the camp.

SUPERSTITION

If a person sincerely believes in something, then the object of his belief has become a reality—at least for him. So, in a sense, the definition of superstition depends, at best, on an external evaluation. The participant is a believer. He is convinced of the validity of the object of his belief. The skeptic may look on and ridicule, but he is doing so from the perspective of his own value system. He doesn't believe; therefore, for instance, to apply holy water to an open sore is blatant stupidity to him. But this is not so for the devout disciple who reaches into the slimy turtle pond and with hope and faith fills his little bottle. The world views of believer and agnostic part as ships passing in the night.

We must be sympathetic with the devotee who, out of a heart-hunger for God, has been led down a path that the Christian regards as false. What if the Christian had had only the opportunities that most mystics have in regard to understanding the truth and light of the gospel? Few folk Muslims have received a relevant explanation of salvation in Christ.

On the other hand, we as Christians do have an objective guide by which we can and must judge error from truth. The Bible is a universal expression of God's will for man. When folk Islam is evaluated biblically it is found seriously wanting. So, although we do so sympathetically, we must speak the truth—with love.

Idries Shah comments on the excesses of belief in *pirs*.

> The Sufi teacher is a conductor and an instructor—not a god. Personality-worship is forbidden in Sufism. Hence Rumi: "Look not at my exterior form, but take what is in my hand;" and Gurgani: "My humility which you mention is not there for you to be impressed by it. It is there for its own reason." Yet such is the attraction of personality to the ordinary man that the successors of Sufi teachers have tended to produce, rather than a living application of the principles taught, hagiographies and bizarre and deficient systems. The theme of the temporary nature of the "cocoon" is conveniently forgotten.[2]

How do we evaluate all the myths that build up around a *pir?* These relate to miracles, chronological age, and so many other areas. The *pir* is perceived as a superman. Perhaps ordinary man well understands his own weakness and therefore desires to relate to strength. He receives a vicarious satisfaction from being part of a particular *tarika* that is led by a strong, dynamic personality. It is wise for the Christian to realize this same thing often occurs as people flock to a church that is pastored by a colorful, charismatic leader. But personality worship is to be condemned whether it is found in folk Islam or Christianity. God will share His glory with no man.

A distraught Muslim wrote this letter to the editor of a large newspaper.

> Recently a pious Muslim lady died of a tumor without taking any recourse to treatment because her *pir* said that if she placed herself under medical or surgical treatment, it would cause harm to her sons who were at that moment in foreign lands for study and service. The poor lady put implicit faith in the saying of the *pir* and embraced death without disclosing her ailment to anybody outside her immediate close family unit. At the last moment she was removed to the hospital and the cause of death was detected. She may not be alone in falling victim to the unholy clutches of a so-called *pir*. Many others may have followed her way. It is time that we become alert and save innocent people from an untimely and agonizing death.[3]

Faith should have a rational basis. Blind faith can lead one down a path of destruction, as was the case with this particular Muslim lady. There should be a distinction made between a respected religious teacher and the commonly-found *pir*. The former points away from himself to God. He seeks no personal exaltation. It is legitimate for him to suggest prayer to obtain physical, spiritual, and emotional healing, but the teacher would not give counsel that opposes medical science. He sees God as responding to a prayer of faith as well as working through the hands of a skilled surgeon. Unfortunately, the *pir* often basks in the glory of all the praise heaped upon him by his initiated disciples. He slowly begins to see himself as a person of great power and wisdom. The unskilled use of such authority over man leads to the excesses we find in mystical Islam. The *pir* is vulnerable particularly in cases that involve physical healing. His advice to the sick may be to drink holy water or to just wear amulets that contain Quranic verses. If such counsel fails to bring healing, the *pir* will simply shrug and say that whatever happened was the will of God.

Such an unquestioning faith is capsulated in these words:

> Fortunate and happy are those that get attached to the *pirs* of the world and happiest is the seeker that can say inwardly to his *pir*, "As thou wishest, so let it be. Only let me remember all the while that thou wishest so;" and later on, "But if for the fulfillment of thy purposes, thou wishest to induce in me the beginning of thyself, let it be so too."[4]

It is dangerous for a disciple to say to his *pir*, "As thou wishest, so let it be." I am reminded of the shock experienced when the news flashes about Jonestown came over television. The cameras slowly panned the rows upon rows of corpses. A mother clutching a baby, a child huddled up to a father—all the victims of faith in an unworthy leader who declared he was God's special agent of revelation. Jim Jones had attracted primarily the poor and unschooled. Often *pirs* attract a similar group of people. Superstition breeds most quickly among the ignorant. Yet, there are significant exceptions where the rich and highly educated become disciples. They also can be victims of superstition, but in many instances they are simply expressing a hunger for a greater spiritual reality. We must constantly remember that the *pirs* portray themselves as specially empowered men of God and therefore worthy of complete trust.

A critical word needs to be said concerning the financial dealing of many *pirs*. Consider one instance: "A young *pir*, who had passed his B.A. set out on a six weeks' tour to visit his *murids*. He returned with twenty sheep and goats, six cows, and rupees six hundred in cash."[5]

One of the recurring criticisms of mystical leaders relates to finances. Seldom is there a system of accountability for the collections that are made in the name of a *pir*, departed or alive. I have seen huge amounts of money being dropped in a hole in the top of a large steel container during the *urs* of one famous departed *pir*. These disciples are convinced they will receive an earthly and a heavenly reward as a result of their sacrificial gift. The local keepers of the money delight to use the offerings to purchase marijuana and other mind-altering drugs. This represents quite a contrast between belief and action of giver and recipient!

The donations made at a *mazar* or during an *urs* are collected by the caretakers of the site. It would be unrealistic to think that such large sums are needed to keep the shrine in good repair. Rather, it is obvious that certain people are exploiting the followers and misappropriating this money in the name of religion.

Pirs usually do not charge for their services, but devotees are expected to give substantially to the *pir* as a thank offering for his concern and prayers. Many *pirs* have small schools which they operate as part of their ministry. Some feed the poor, particularly on the occasion of their annual meeting. However, there are extremely wealthy and influential *pirs* who seem to be very greedy. These are the men who are charged with hypocritically using religion as a convenient way to conduct business. The nonbeliever may objectively evaluate these *pirs* as frauds and deceivers—but devotees continue to fill the coffers.

While visiting one Muslim country, I was able to interview a brilliant retired professor who has intensively researched Sufism and has produced an excellent book on the history, doctrine, and practices of Sufism. It is not prudent to reveal his identity, but I copied some of his comments into my notebook while we chatted.

> Almost all Muslims in this country are worshipers of *pirs*. Only very few Muslims are orthodox. . . . Imams who are connected to *mazars* only support the *pir's* memory for financial reasons. . . . There is no relationship between orthodox Muslims and *pirs* and Sufis. I would like to go to the *mazars* and kick them, but I won't because I'm afraid I would lose my neck. . . . DAMN THE *PIRS!*

In the same country, the president, prime minister, and chief of the armed forces visited a certain immensely popular *pir* to seek his blessing. This *pir* has several hundred thousand people attending his annual gathering. Needless to say, it is expedient for politicians to pay respect to such a leader—whether or not they are sympathetic to his religious views.

A good, succinct critique of Sufi excesses has been penned by the Islamics expert, Kenneth Cragg.

> "Come where I am; I can show you the way" is the mystic's call to man, not: "Believe what I teach, I can tell you the orthodox truth." As such the Sufi represents at once a protest, an aspiration, and a goal. His very lack of rational concern and some of the forms of his technique are liable to lead him into aberration and bring his purpose into disrepute. Some Sufi doctrines of passivity and the Sufi veneration of saints have occasioned no little apathy and crude superstition. Sufism has suffered from its own excesses and is reproached by many modern reformers.[6]

THE TEACHING ABOUT ABSORPTION

William Wells, former professor at Wheaton Graduate School, has written concerning the Sufi doctrine of absorption:

> Mysticism is often divided into mysticism of communion and mysticism of absorption. The first is entirely compatible with the Christian (and Western) distinction between the Creator and the created. It doesn't move me much personally, but I have no theological objections. The second undermines that most fundamental distinction. Nevertheless, it has been found in the West within all three major Western religious traditions. However, mysticism of absorption is more characteristic of the Eastern religious tradition. Sufism, in my understanding, is of the second type. It would be, therefore, fundamentally incompatible with Muslim thought. Why don't Sufis recognize that incompatibility?[7]

Wells has accurately assessed a fundamental distinction between folk Islam and orthodox Islam. That is why mystics of past ages have been maligned by the fundamentalists within Islam. But there is a distinction to be drawn between excesses of teaching, which cross an unseen boundary and tumble into heresy, and a more benign presentation of the same or a similar belief. For instance, few Christians would say a believer ever spiritually merges into God, but they have no difficulty affirming that God comes into a believer and takes up a pervasive and permanent residence within the heart. The former belief system seems radical while the latter has been accepted by millions of Christians down through the ages. In both instances, the central teaching is the establishment of a meaningful relationship between God and man.

A Muslim friend of mine has sent his two sons to a *pir* in order that this man who is reputed to possess great spiritual power may breathe upon them. This exercise is supposed to assist the boys to study for upcoming exams. The belief is that, in a mystical manner, God is in that puff of air that is coming from the body of the *pir.* So, here we have a commonly accepted practice meant to ensure that one is filled with the presence and power of God.

Folk Muslims enjoy the ambivalence and vagaries of Islam. It allows them to be at times mildly heretical and at other times grossly inconsistent. Some mystics believe in assimilation, others in being filled with God, and still others claim a more external spiritual influence. This apparent lack of unified teaching is of no real consequence to the mystic.

A Muslim has interestingly written of what he perceives to be the meaning of Christian baptism as compared with the teaching of Sufis on absorption into God.

> The water symbolizes the ocean in which there are so many waves and yet it is one ocean. Baptism means immersion in this spiritual ocean, which is the Spirit of God, and becoming as nothing, in the love of God, in the knowledge of God, and in the realization of God. From that time one understands the meaning of the saying, "I exist no more as myself, as

a separate entity; and yet I exist, and this existence is the existence of God."

This is the main teaching of Sufism: to sink into the consciousness of God, that no trace of one's limited being may be found, at least in one's consciousness. That is really the ideal, the path, and the goal of all.[8]

It is most instructive to observe how this Muslim writer has used Galatians 2:20 ("I have been crucified with Christ; and it is no longer I who live, but Christ lives in me; and the life which I now live in the flesh I live by faith in the Son of God, who loved me and delivered Himself up for me") as a proof text for Sufism. He simply extends the Christian belief of being filled and controlled by God into a further and final stage—that of absorption into the Divine Being.

Whether or not the Sufi can distinguish between absorption and being filled with God is an important point to the Christian. This teaching about absorption, taken to its logical conclusion, ends with man as God. The merger becomes complete. Man is no longer recognizable as a separate entity, but rather has become an incarnation of God. This belief completely undercuts the truth that man is a sinner who stands in desperate need of the reconciling and redeeming work of the Savior, Jesus Christ. Therefore, folk Muslims must be brought to a point where they can see that their legitimate spiritual needs can be met only in Christ, rather than in a psychological exercise based on false teaching.

NOTES

1. Hazrat Inayat Khan, *The Sufi Message of Hazrat Inayat Khan* (London: Barrie and Rockliff, 1963), vol. 9, 256.

2. Idries Shah, *The Way of the Sufi* (New York: Dutton, 1970), 31.

3. H. Rahman, "Anomalies," in Reader's Forum of *The* [Dacca] *New Nation* (March 15, 1981), 5.

4. Hira Lal Chapra, "Sufism," in *The Cultural Heritage of India*, ed. Haridas Bhattacharyya, vol. 4, *The Religions* (Calcutta: Ramakrishna Mission Institute of Culture, 1956), 609.

5. Violet Rhoda Jones and L. Bevan Jones, *Woman in Islam* (Lucknow: Lucknow Publishing House, 1941), 363.

6. Kenneth Cragg, *The Call of the Minaret* (New York: Oxford University, 1956), 135.

7. William Wells, personal letter to the author (May 20, 1981), 1.

8. Khan, *The Sufi Message*, vol. 9, 188.

5

$$\longleftarrow\!\!\!\!\!-\!\!\!\!\!\longrightarrow\!\!\!\bowtie\!\!\longleftarrow\!\!\!\!\!-\!\!\!\!\!\longrightarrow$$

BRIDGES TO MYSTICAL ISLAM

Bridges are a necessary part of life. Even in ancient times, primitive man built bridges to assist him in movement. The special thing about bridges is that they are instruments of bringing together that which is separated. A few years ago, I journeyed from Asia to Europe. Actually, it wasn't difficult. It required only a ride across the bridge in Istanbul that spans the Straits. How important this bridge is for the purpose of linking two continents together.

Bridges are also valuable in a religious sense. They can function as connectors between people of entirely diverse viewpoints and world views. Islam and Christianity can be likened to two continents opposite each other. Antagonism, suspicion, and even hatred swirl in the raging waters that separate the two. A few brave people have set out in small boats in an attempt to cross over to the other bank with a message of peace, understanding, and sensitivity. A few of these boats have crossed safely; others have been swept away in the tumultuous current.

What is needed is a new structure to bridge the gap. Islam has listened, observed, and evaluated. Christianity has been found wanting. There is much validity in the Muslim judgment. This chapter will seek to explore reasons for the distance that remains between Muslims and Christians, as well as postulate suggestions for closing the gap.

THE MUSLIM PERCEPTION OF CHRISTIANITY

Do we really want to understand how others perceive us? It can be a painful process. The difference between how we see ourselves and how others see us can be immense. Remembering that folk Muslims are very much within the worldwide community of Muslims, let us examine some of the root causes of antagonism by looking at pivotal points in history.

622—Islam experienced a bloody birth as Muhammad fled Mecca and found refuge in Medina. His subsequent battles and victories established Islam as a dominant religious and political force in Saudi Arabia.

632–750—The death of the Prophet in 632 served to inspire his followers to move from the Arabian desert and to make overwhelming conquests in the Middle East and North Africa. The Christian church in this area flickered out, with the exception of the Coptic church in Egypt.

750–1100—Islam sparkled into a cultural and intellectual force. Muslims, during this so-called Golden Age, excelled in science and in the arts. I have visited museums and mosques in Istanbul and Damascus. The artifacts from this historical period are exceedingly beautiful.

1100–1450—European soldiers on horseback slowly skirted the northern shores of the Mediterranean into Lebanon, finally reaching the "holy land." Several years ago, I toured this area and was able to go inside several of the Crusader fortresses which even today are in excellent condition. Between Beirut, Sidon, and Tyre, a number of forts stand on small man-made islands just off the mainland. I relived the experiences of these "pious" soldiers who had painted the sign of the cross on their breastplates and saddles. On Sundays, for a brief period, they would lay aside their task of slaughtering Muslims and participate in a time of fervent worship and petition, asking the Lord Jesus to assist them in their conquests. Fierce battles raged between the followers of Christ and the Sons of Ishmael. Control of Palestine and particularly Jerusalem shifted between these two opposing forces a number of times during these years. At the end of the eight Crusades, antagonism between adherents of the two religions had cemented. The memory of this dark stain on church history remains fresh and vivid for millions of Muslims.

1700–1960—Colonialism, to the Muslim, meant that more than ninety percent of his co-religionists were, at some time during this period, subject to "Christian" foreign rule. How demeaning for an orthodox Muslim to be forced to submit to the authority of a white-faced foreigner who at least nominally adhered to a religion regarded as antithetical to Islam. The memory of this age of subjugation burns deep in Muslims today.

1945–1970—The Second World War served as a springboard for the independence movement among Muslim countries. The modus operandi varied from rational negotiations to violent confrontations. But did the nations of Islam really become free of foreign influence? In some cases, these countries were forced to continue to look westward for economic assistance—with all the attendant political obligations.

1970 to the present—Discovery! Muslim countries convulsed the world overnight by driving oil prices to phenomenal heights. Suddenly Muslims obtained a new sense of identity. They had now arrived in the community of nations. No longer would they be obsequious. Their posture would be one of strength.

As one carefully reviews Muslim-Christian relations from a historical perspective, it becomes clear why the few extreme leaders in the Muslim world can obtain a dedicated following. It is important to note that not all Muslims approve of religious fanaticism. Many of my friends are deeply embarrassed over events in Libya and Iran. Yet that doesn't mean that the more rational Muslims are drawn toward Christianity. It only means that they disagree with Christians and Christianity in a more sane manner.

Now let us examine perception on a more limited basis. How does it relate to individuals? A pertinent illustration is that of the missionaries who lived in the old-style compounds in India.

> In India the missionaries were called *dore*. The word is used for rich farmers and small-time kings. These petty rulers bought large pieces of land, put up compound walls, built bungalows, and had servants. They also erected separate

bungalows for their second and third wives. When the missionaries came they bought large pieces of land, put up compound walls, built bungalows, and had servants. They, too, erected separate bungalows, but for the missionary ladies stationed on the same compound.

Missionary wives were called *dorasani*. The term is used not for the wife of a *dore*, for she should be kept in isolation away from the public eye, but his mistress whom he often took with him in his cart or car.

The problem here is one of cross-cultural misunderstanding. The missionary thought of himself as a "missionary," not realizing that there is no such thing in the traditional Indian society. In order to relate to him the people had to find him a role within their own set of roles, and they did so. Unfortunately the missionaries were not aware of how the people perceived them.[1]

My research on this subject has led me to a startling conclusion. The missionary is often perceived by the Muslim community as nothing more than an efficient secular administrator. He has great resources available and is able to effectively initiate and complete programs. This was brought home to me in a powerful, painful manner a few years ago. At that time I was renting office space from a very high-placed Muslim government official. We had many talks together on a great variety of subjects. One day he piercingly looked at me and said, "Mr. Parshall, are you a man of God like my friend Mr. Lakin?" That question caught me off guard. Mr. Lakin, a missionary colleague, looks, acts, and talks like one of God's special saints. Regaining my composure, I sought to assure the official of my theological orthodoxy. After a few moments of reflection, he quietly said, "But Mr. Parshall, you are more like an American diplomat." What a contrast in perception! I was being perceived merely as being informed, articulate, and dynamic, whereas my desire was to be perceived as godly and humble. That encounter led me to study how Muslim priests and Christian missionaries are frequently perceived in society (see table 1).

Table 1

POPULAR PERCEPTIONS OF MUSLIM PRIESTS AND CHRISTIAN MISSIONARIES

	Muslim Priest	**Christian Missionary**
Image	Passive disposition	Energetic—a doer
	Subjective outlook	Objective orientation to life
	People-oriented	Task-oriented
	Financially poor (with the exception of certain *pirs)*	Regarded as wealthy—possesses a car, camera, tape recorder
	Does not attend theater, watch television, or go to movies	Does all of these
	Does not eat in expensive restaurants	Eats in expensive restaurants (at least occasionally)
	Does not eat pork	Eats pork
	Clothing identifies him as a religious person	Clothing identifies him as a secular person
	Wears a beard	Infrequently has a beard
	Wife wears a veil or modest, culturally-approved clothing	Wife does not always dress in clothing that Muslims consider modest; thus missionary wives are identified with the "sinful" actresses seen in Western movies and television series
Ministry	Mosque is focus of life	Goes to church a few hours per week
	Prays publicly five times a day	Rarely prays in public
	Fasts for one month during daylight hours	Seldom, if ever, fasts
	Constantly uses religious vocabulary	Rarely uses religious vocabulary

Table 1 (cont.)

	Muslim Priest	Christian Missionary
Ministry (cont.)	Does not distribute relief funds or financial aid; receives local money only	Dispenses funds from foreign sources—in the form of relief funds, jobs, training institutions, hospitals
	Has no employees	Has employees and thus acquires status
	Puts little value on non-Quranic education	Puts great value on formal, secular education and degrees
	Memorizes vast parts of the Quran in Arabic	Memorizes very little of the Bible—in any language
	Involves himself in a ministry of healing—pours consecrated water on a sick person, puts charms on the diseased, chants the Quran, says prayers	Emphasizes the scientific, not the spiritual—offers a mild prayer for the sick with little faith or conviction; people go to the missionary for medicine, not prayer

Many of these perceptions are shared by folk Muslims as well as the orthodox.

We ignore this data to our peril. It does matter what Muslims think of Christians—and particularly what they think of those who are committed to the propagation of the gospel. There are many facets to effective cross-cultural communication, which is a complicated process. It is simply not possible for a Westerner to become an Easterner. But such a reality does not preclude making the distance as minimal as possible.

FELT NEEDS

The mystic, above all, wants to know his Beloved. The ultimate experience is to be intoxicated with God. How similar this desire is to that of the psalmist as he records his hunger for the Lord.

> As the deer pants for the water brooks,
> So my soul pants for Thee, O God.
> My soul thirsts for God, for the living God.
> (Psalm 42:1–2)

> O God, Thou art my God; I shall seek Thee earnestly:
> My soul thirsts for Thee, my flesh yearns for Thee,
> In a dry and weary land where there is no water.
> (Psalm 63:1)

> My soul longed and even yearned for the courts of the LORD;
> My heart and my flesh sing for joy to the living God.
> (Psalm 84:2)

Charles R. Marsh, writing from an African context, sees both the Christian and the Muslim as desiring a relationship with the Creator.

> It is clear that in the hearts of many African men, be they animists, Muslims, or Christians, there is a reaching out for the mystical and unseen, and God can use this deep desire, even when it is debased and primitive, to prepare a man or woman to drink of the living streams.[2]

The forms of folk Islam are all directed toward this mystical experience. Singing gustily with head turned upward and eyes closed takes the devotee into another world. Mystics who sit in a circle and pass around the water pipe *(hooka)* filled with marijuana are taking a "trip" into the cosmos. There, for a brief moment, they are merging into the Divine. *Dhikr* provides another ecstatic experience with God. The emotional repetition of the names of God lifts one into the heavens. Without doubt, the majority of folk Muslims seek a mystical encounter with God.

Table 2

POPULAR ISLAM: FELT-NEEDS, ANIMISTIC, AND POSSIBLE CHRISTIAN ANSWERS[3]

Felt-Needs in Popular Islam	Animistic Answers to Felt-Needs Not Acceptable to More Acceptable			Christian Answers to Felt-Needs
fear of unknown	idolatry stone worship	fetishes talismans charms	superstition	security in Christ as Guide, Keeper
fear of evil	sorcery witchcraft	amulets knots	exorcism	exorcism, protection in Christ
fear of the future	angel worship	divination spells	fatalism fanaticism	trust in Christ as Lord of the future
shame of not being in the group	magic curse or bless	hair or nail trimmings		acceptance in fellowship of believers
powerlessness of individual against evil	saint worship		baraka saint/angel petitioning	authority and power of the Holy Spirit
meaningless-ness of life		familiar spirit		purpose in life as God's child
sickness	tree/saint worship	healing magic		divine healing

Bill Musk, an astute observer of African folk Islam, has constructed a chart (see table 2) to highlight felt needs of mystical Muslims. A few categories apply only to African Islam, but the chart is a good overview of popular Islam.

As Musk shows, one recurrent problem is fear: fear of the unknown, fear of the future, fear of evil, and fear of sickness. Historically, mystics have sought to shift emphasis from the fear of God to the love of God.

To some extent, they have been successful. Their poems, songs, and preaching center on the theme of love. But my observation is that, on the grassroots level, there is pervasive fear. Each little hamlet, every small village contains scores of people weighed down under the heavy burden of fear.

> Of greater concern and preoccupation are the Muslim's efforts to cope with the various acute problems and hostile forces which crowd his world and keep him from peace of mind and heart. There is the magic he feels he must practice. And what of the demons he must placate? Or the fetishes he must not fail to use? Will his invoking of the saints help him surmount his fears? On and on. His world is dominated by the "evil eye," by sickness and death, by sorcery and curses. Not by Quranic Islam but by animistic Islam, and the hunger of the heart it constantly discloses.[4]

Fear is a continual, strong force that moves the mystic toward animistic and, at times, esoteric practices. His heart-hunger is for release. On the other hand, what about love? Has the mystic been able to drown in the swirling currents of the ocean of God's love? Has fear been overcome by the emphasis on the wine of love dispensed by the gracious tavernkeeper?

Folk Muslims think of love in most subjective terms. It is what is good, beautiful, benign, and artistic. It is to be enjoyed. It is self-centered as well as God-centered. It is, above all, free and liberating. Love—the queen of all virtues. "In the end it was this mystical love, so close in its conceptions and language to the primitive Christian Mysticism, which reduced the ascetic motive of fear to the second place, and supplied the basis for Sufism."[5]

> It is because of this element of love that Sufism has been the source of vitality to Islam. It bears out the truth of what someone has said, "Dogma and duty are not the whole of a religion." There are, in our nature, needs of loving and of suffering, as well as of believing and of doing; and no faith that does not contain something to satisfy these needs could

ever have wielded that vast power which, as a matter of fact, has been and is being exercised by Muhammadanism.[6]

Another need clearly seen among folk Muslims is that of fellowship. One seldom finds mystics alone for an extended period of time. A few, with extreme meditative tendencies, will go off into isolated places. They are the exceptions. The norm is an intensely personal intercourse between mystics. The tie between *pir* and disciple is proverbial. As mentioned earlier, the devotee is required to follow the advice of his spiritual guide at all costs. This relationship becomes equal to if not greater than that of blood kinship.

> The whole Sufi community forms one indivisible brotherhood, so that the meanest [devotee] feels himself to be joined in spirit with the most exalted hierophant. The Sufis look upon themselves as God's chosen people, loved by Him and loving one another in Him; and the bond between them can never be broken, for it is a marriage of true souls, which was made in heaven.[7]

One of the most recurrent of all felt needs involves healing. All people in the world regard illness as an undesirable reality. The Christian usually responds to sickness with a dash to the medicine cabinet followed by a prayer to God for healing. The folk Muslims reaction to illness is often of a more mystical nature. He will go to his *pir* so that the *pir* may breathe upon his body. Holy water will be drunk. Amulets with Quranic verses of healing potency will be worn. Magical formulas will be repeated. Promises of donations to a special saint will be made. Fervent prayer will be offered in the name of a departed *pir.*

How does the Christian respond to this and other needs of the mystic community? This next section will seek to identify ways to answer the cries of the folk Muslim.

METHODS OF MEETING FELT NEEDS

In *Muslim Evangelism*, I listed seven areas that could serve as bridges between Sufism and Christianity.

1. The Sufi view of God. Allah is above all and totally in control of His creation.
2. The Sufi stress on a personal relationship with God.
3. The de-emphasis of the value of ritual and form.
4. The necessity of a hunger for God.
5. An awareness of the working of God's grace in the lives of men and women.
6. A similar goal of being with God one day.
7. A belief in intermediaries between God and man. This is a natural bridge to an effective presentation of Jesus as mediator for estranged mankind.[8]

And now we will take up in some detail these suggestions as well as others.

THEOLOGICAL SIMILARITIES

A high view of monotheism dominates almost all mystical thought. The only exception would be Hindu-influenced Sufism which, if it led to polytheism, would be considered anomalous to the main stream of Sufi belief. It is on the important point of belief in one God that Muslims and Christians agree.

The most common form of *dhikr* is the recital of the ninety-nine names of God. To facilitate this repetition, the worshiper uses a rosary of ninety-nine beads. The origin of this practice is thought to lie with the Buddhists. Use of a rosary is a common phenomenon throughout the Muslim world; history indicates that Roman Catholics adopted the practice from Muslims (c. 1100).

There are several lists of the ninety-nine names of God. It is quite exciting to read and meditate on these names. Most of them can be fully accepted by believers in the Old and New Testaments. This certainly sets the stage for dialogue and witness. It is an excellent beginning to discuss what some of these names—such as The Merciful, The Pardoner, The Judge, The All-Loving, The First, and The Last—mean. In the list that follows the left-hand column contains the Arabic; its English equivalent is on the right.

1. Rahman   The Compassionate
2. Rahim   The Merciful
3. Malik   The King
4. Quddus   The Holy One
5. Salam   The Peace
6. Momin   The Faithful
7. Mohymin   The Protector
8. Aziz   The Incomparable
9. Jabbar   The Benefactor
10. Mutakabbir   The Mighty Doer
11. Khaliq   The Creator
12. Bari   The Maker
13. Musawwir   The Former
14. Ghafar   The Forgiver
15. Qahhar   The Powerful
16. Wahhab   The Giver
17. Razzaq   The Bestower of Daily Bread
18. Fattah   The Opener
19. Alim   The Omniscient
20. Qabiz   The Restrainer
21. Basit   The Expander
22. Khafiz   The Depresser
23. Rafi   The Exalter
24. Muiz   The Strengthener
25. Muzil   The Lowerer
26. Sami   The Hearer
27. Basir   The Seer
28. Hakam   The Judge
29. Adl   The Just
30. Latif   The Benignant
31. Khabir   The Knower
32. Halim   The Clement

33.	Azim	The Great
34.	Ghafur	The Great Pardoner
35.	Shakur	The Rewarder
36.	Ali	The Most High
37.	Kabir	The Great Lord
38.	Hafiz	The Guardian
39.	Muqit	The Giver of Strength
40.	Hasib	The Reckoner
41.	Jalil	The Glorious
42.	Karim	The Munificent
43.	Raqib	The Watcher
44.	Mujib	The Approver of Supplications
45.	Wasi	The Expander
46.	Hakim	The Physician
47.	Wadud	The All-Loving
48.	Majid	The Glorious
49.	Bais	The Awakener
50.	Shahid	The Witness
51.	Haqq	The True
52.	Wakil	The Provider
53.	Qawwi	The Powerful
54.	Matin	The Firm
55.	Wali	The Friend
56.	Hamid	The One to Be Praised
57.	Muhsi	The Counter
58.	Mubdi	The Cause
59.	Muid	The Restorer
60.	Mohyi	The Life-Giver
61.	Mumit	The Death-Giver
62.	Hai	The Living
63.	Qaiyyum	The Self-Subsisting
64.	Wajid	The Finder
65.	Majid	The Grand
66.	Wahid	The Unique
67.	Samad	The Perpetual

68. Qadir	The Powerful
69. Muqtadir	The Prevailing
70. Muqaddim	The Bringer Before
71. Muwakhkhir	The Bringer After
72. Awwal	The First
73. Akhir	The Last
74. Zahir	The Evident
75. Batin	The Hidden
76. Wali	The Governor
77. Muta'a	The Sublime
78. Barr	The Doer of Good
79. Tawwab	The Propitious
80. Muntaqim	The Avenger
81. Afu	The Eraser
82. Rauf	The Benefiter
83. Malik-ul-Mulk	The King of Kingdoms
84. Zuljalal-wal-Ikram	The Lord of Glory and Honor
85. Muksit	The Equitable
86. Jami	The Assembler
87. Ghani	The Rich
88. Maghani	The Enricher
89. Muti	The Giver
90. Mani	The Withholder
91. Zarr	The Afflicter
92. Nafi	The Benefactor
93. Nur	The Light
94. Hadi	The Guide
95. Badia	The Incomparable
96. Baqi	The Eternal
97. Waris	The Inheritor
98. Rashid	The Director
99. Sabur	The Patient[9]

It is scriptural to meditate upon God and on His Holy Word. The Lord commanded Joshua that "this book of the law shall not depart from your mouth, but you shall meditate on it day and night, so that you may be careful to do according to all that is written in it" (Joshua 1:8).

Longing for God is an area of compatibility between Christians and Muslims. Rabia-al-Adwiyya, in 802, penned these heart-searching words: "O my Lord, if I worship Thee from fear of Hell, burn me in Hell, if I worship Thee from hope of Paradise, exclude me thence, but if I worship Thee for Thine own sake, then withhold not from me Thine eternal beauty."[10] The mystic's hunger for a personal relationship with the Lord opens a door for sharing Christ as the one who can bridge the distance between sinner and God.

The mystic is a strong believer in prayer. Abd-al-Masih, a missionary to Muslims for fifty years, gives his impressions of the Islamic prayer ritual.

> Together they recited the first chapter of the Quran: "In the name of Allah, the Gracious, the Merciful. All praise belongs to Allah, Lord of all the worlds. The Gracious, The Merciful, Master of the Day of Judgment. Thee alone do we worship, and Thee alone do we implore for help. Guide us in the right path, the path of those on whom Thou has bestowed Thy blessings, those who have not incurred Thy displeasure, and those who have not gone astray."

> The sheikh said, "God is great" and bent down until his forehead touched the ground. The men did the same after him. In this position they said,

> "Glory be to God the Lord of the Universe."

> Then they stood and said,

> "God hears those who praise Him."

> Three times they bowed themselves saying,

> "Glory to God the Lord most high."

> Kneeling and raising their heads they cried, "God is great."

Then they recited,

"O God, forgive me, have pity on me, direct me aright, preserve me and make me great. Strengthen my faith and enrich me . . . ."

At last the prayer was finished. Each man turned his head, first to the right, then to the left, and saluted the angels saying the age-long formula,

"Peace be unto you." "Peace be unto you."

As Abd-al-Masih watched, he was deeply moved. There was something uncanny, deeply mystical, yet profoundly impressive in this early morning prayer. He could not do otherwise than respect this solemn observance of prayer, the acknowledgement of the one God. For many of these men it expressed a true desire, a deep yearning for God.[11]

The Muslim observes the Christian and asks why he doesn't pray. It is very difficult for him to understand the Christian's hesitancy to pray in public. It is my firm belief that prayer can be a bond—and a catalyst for witness—between sincere Muslims and followers of Christ. There is so much in the Islamic prayer ritual, both actual and symbolic, that can be appreciated by Christians.

Years ago, my wife and I were invited to the home of a very influential Muslim family for tea. Everyone was friendly and gracious. At dusk, all rose and excused themselves to go into an inner room to pray. My wife and I sat on the couch feeling a bit awkward talking about trivial matters while the Muslims were inside praying to Allah. But weren't we the missionaries who possessed the real truth about God? I decided at that time that I would not let this occur in my home.

This same Muslim family has become very intimate with us. When they visit us, at prayer time, I go into a private room with my friend. We put down the prayer mats and I kneel beside him in silent petition while he goes through the prescribed Muslim ritual. At the end he prays a very fervent extemporaneous prayer.

I then pray, finishing in Jesus' name. My friend is deeply impressed that I will pray with him. He fully understands our theological distinctions. There is no question of religious syncretism. But there is an appreciation that I too sincerely want to know and follow God. This has opened up many meaningful opportunities for witness.

The person and teachings of Jesus Christ are appreciated by mystics. "Moreover Sufis hold that the Lord Jesus is of all the Divine Envoys *(rusul)* the most perfect type of contemplative saint. To offer the left cheek to him who smites one on the right is true spiritual detachment; it is a voluntary withdrawal from the interplay of cosmic actions and reactions."[12]

Like Gandhi of India, mystics are impressed with the teachings of the Sermon on the Mount. The high moral and ethical standards elucidated in these Scriptures are similar to what folk Muslims believe should be the behavior of mankind.

The most important bridge is the mediatorial role of Christ. He stands between God and man as friend, guide, comforter, and, most importantly, as Savior. To many Muslims this type of mediator is the person of Muhammad. "The ideas developed in later Folk Islam concerning the person of Muhammad show a remarkable likeness to what is known in Christian theology as the doctrine of a Mediator."[13] But, on a folk or popular level, mystics actually look to their *pirs,* departed or alive, as the specially empowered saints who can act as mediators for them. These saints are said to intercede in much the same manner as Christ does for the believer.

> I pray for them. I am not praying for the world, but for those you have given me, for they are yours. (John 17:9 NIV)

> Holy Father, protect them by the power of your name. (John 17:11 NIV)

> My prayer is not that you take them out of the world but that you protect them from the evil one. They are not of the world,

even as I am not of it. Sanctify them by the truth; your word
is truth. (John 17:15–17 NIV)

Father, I want those you have given me to be with me where
I am, and to see my glory. (John 17:24 NIV)

A verse that has pungency in witness to folk Muslims is 1 Timothy
2:5–6 NIV:

For there is one God and one mediator between God and
men, the man Christ Jesus, who gave himself as a ransom
for all men.

Here is a clear reference to the *one* mediator. The multiplicity of
mediators between God and men is denied. Questions will then arise as
to who Jesus Christ really was. What does it mean to give oneself for
others? The *pirs* only dispense holy water, amulets, and advice . . . and
that often for the purpose of monetary gain. Christ, in stark contrast,
has no hidden agenda. His act of giving was without self-interest. The
next query concerning this verse is in regard to the word *ransom*. Here a
whole range of subjects opens itself to the Christian communicator, for
using the term *ransom* leads to making cross-references to original sin;
the condemnation which lies upon all men; Jesus as a sinless substitute
for the sinner; the death and resurrection of Christ; and the forgiveness
the confessing sinner finds in the work of the atonement.

I have never met a Muslim who could assure me that he knew he
was going to heaven when he died. Islam teaches that there are degrees
of rewards in heaven as well as various measures of punishment in hell.
Each time a Muslim prays, he is to pray for the dead, particularly for the
prophets. No living person can be sure of the present state of those who
have died. Muslims often articulate their personal fear of death. They
can only hope their good deeds outweigh the evil they have done. The
following verses have been effective in causing Muslims to realize the
inadequacy of their soteriology.

Therefore, there is now no condemnation for those who are in
Christ Jesus. (Romans 8:1 NIV)

Know that a man is not justified by observing the law, but by
faith in Jesus Christ. (Galatians 2:16 NIV)

"Death has been swallowed up in victory. Where, O death,
is your victory? Where, O death, is your sting?" The sting of
death is sin, and the power of sin is the law. But thanks be to
God! He gives us the victory through our Lord Jesus Christ.
(1 Corinthians 15:54–57 NIV)

I write these things to you who believe in the name of the
Son of God so that you may know that you have eternal life.
(1 John 5:13 NIV)

The three key words in the passage from 1 John are *believe, know,*
and *have.* These concepts have been very powerful in communicating
assurance to folk Muslims. It is easy to convince mystics of the inadequacy
of the law. They are fully aware that the law condemns but gives no
power to overcome the flesh. Mystics are looking for a relationship with
God that leads to assurance of eternal life. This, uniquely, we can offer in
the liberating message of the gospel of Christ.

Love is a supracultural truth. This concept is part of every religion in
the world. The word is often caricatured and made into a gross distortion
of that which God intended. In the world today one can "love" God or
"love" a prostitute. It is indeed sad that one word can be used to describe
a heavenly encounter as well as a fleshly tryst.

Man acknowledges the need to love and be loved, both on a human
and a divine level. To the mystic, love is the very core of his being.
Hate is the antithesis of all he stands for. Many folk Muslims have been
gripped by biblical references such as these:

See how great a love the Father has bestowed upon us, that
we should be called the children of God. (1 John 3:1)

Every one who loves is born of God and knows God. (1 John
4:7)

By this the love of God was manifested in us, that God has
sent His only begotten Son into the world so that we might

live through Him. In this is love, not that we loved God, but that He loved us and sent His son to be the propitiation for our sins. Beloved, if God so loves us, we also ought to love one another. (1 John 4:9–11)

So there is a necessity to point out that love is the motivation for God's divine plan for the redemption of sinful man. The mystic will be drawn to Christ as he sees the scope and purpose of the incarnation. Scripture, Christian songs, and poetry can all be effectively used to define love in a meaningful way.

Among mystics, love may be the ideal, but fear is often the norm. The Word of God has much to say in regard to stilling the raging storms of fear that often buffet the soul.

For God has not given us a spirit of timidity, but of power and love and discipline. (2 Timothy 1:7)

The LORD is my light and my salvation; Whom shall I fear: The LORD is the defense of my life; Whom shall I dread? (Psalm 27:1)

The LORD is for me; I will not fear; What can man do to me? (Psalm 118:6)

Peace I leave with you; My peace I give to you; not as the world gives, do I give to you. Let not your heart be troubled, nor let it be fearful. (John 14:27)

Fear is the basis of most psychosomatic illnesses. It is the force that cripples and destroys. Fear breeds in darkness. Oh, the thrill of presenting Christ, the Light of the World, the one who can assist the supplicant in overcoming the dread of enslavement to the forces of fear: the haunting fears of the past; the anxious fears of the present; the enslaving fear of hell—all put under the blood of Christ. Release is more than a romantic ideal; it is an ever-present potential for the humble petitioner.

The Muslim is a person of community. *Tarikas* provide people with a sociological sense of belonging. Christianity should be presented as a warm, loving fellowship of people who care one for another. This has to be more than pious theory. Muslims must see Christian fellowship. This will have a drawing effect. Paul powerfully makes his appeal for this type of community in Philippians 2:1–2:

> If therefore there is any encouragement in Christ, if there is any consolation of love, if there is any fellowship of the Spirit, if any affection and compassion, make my joy complete by being of the same mind, maintaining the same love, united in spirit, intent on one purpose.

The apostle John, writing in 1 John 1:3, speaks of the two dimensions of fellowship:

> What we have seen and heard we proclaim to you also, that you also may have fellowship with us; and indeed our fellowship is with the Father, and with His Son Jesus Christ.

David W. Shenk has given a helpful suggestion on the possibility of using the Book of Hebrews as a bridge in witness.

> Hebrews seems to relate to the spiritual and theological aspirations of Sufi Islam. It quite explicitly recognizes certain socioreligious elements which seem to be similar to aspects of Islamic Sufism. Some of these elements include: An intercessory mediational priesthood. Effective and evidential mediation of grace or blessing. Satisfactory divine-human relationship. Power. Sacrifice and suffering. An alternative cultic community in tension with the larger religious milieu. Progression toward the true knowledge of God so that one can experience inner rest and forgiveness. The mediation of revelation through angels. Obedience to divine law. A recognition of incarnational *Logos* which is, nevertheless, somewhat tempered by the parameters of transcendental monotheism. These and other aspects of the theology of Hebrews suggest that the writer participated in a world view not dissimilar to that of contemporary Sufism. He attempted to interpret life and work of the Messiah into that world view.

The interpretation of the Christian faith and community which is developed by the writer of the Hebrews is both understandable and relevant to people who have accepted the Sufi theological presuppositions with the concurrent *tarika* sociological dynamics. This is not to suggest that Sufi theology is the same as the theology of Hebrews. It is not. But there are redemptive analogies in Sufism and the *tarika* system which the theology of biblical Hebrews may enlarge and fulfill under the enlightening power of the Holy Spirit.[14]

These are a few of the theological potentials for reaching the Muslim mystic.

THE MYSTERY OF THE GOSPEL

Mystics are advocates of the esoteric. They like to feel they have reached out and received something from God that is unique and somewhat removed from the normal stream of human experience. The concepts *mystery* and *secret* are challenging to the folk Muslim. The words *mystic* and *mystery* both come from the Greek root *myst.*

While in North Africa, I was delighted to pick up a book entitled (as I recall) *Seven Secret Steps for Attaining a Knowledge of God.* This small volume was written decades ago by a veteran missionary who was seeking to communicate Christ to the Sufis of North Africa. She had chosen seven as a number that would immediately appeal to Sufis, who believe in moving through seven distinct stages in their quest for God. The word *secret* was attractive, as it suggested the esoteric. This book was a very effective bridge between where the Sufi was in his spiritual pilgrimage and the point to which the missionary wanted to see him progress. Literature of this nature should be carefully prepared and field-tested among folk Muslims throughout the Islamic world.

The Book of Colossians was written with the Gnostic heresy very much in mind. Gnostics were reaching out into the vast unknown for an experience with God. They emphasized that spirit was good and matter evil. They thought that Christ assumed only the appearance of a material form. Man as matter had to overcome evil in order to have a knowledge of God. Gnostics also believed that "there is a long series of emanations between a man and God; man must fight his way up that long ladder to get to God. In order to do that he will need all kinds of secret knowledge and esoteric learning and hidden passwords. He will need an elaborate system of secret and recondite knowledge in order to reach God."[15]

There are similarities between first-century Gnostics and mystical Muslims of the twenty-first century. Therefore, the Book of Colossians can be helpful in presenting the gospel to folk Muslims.

> Of this church I was made a minister according to the steward-ship from God bestowed on me for your benefit, that I might fully carry out the preaching of the word of God, that is, the mystery which has been hidden from the past ages and generations; but has now been manifested to His saints, to whom God willed to make known what is the riches of the glory of this mystery among the Gentiles, which is Christ in you, the hope of glory. (Colossians 1:25–27)

Here we see that which was hidden from past generations of people. But now a select group of people, "the saints," are to be brought into the secret counsels of God. They will be allowed to comprehend "the riches of the glory of this mystery." It is commendable that Paul did not stop at this point and leave the reader grappling with the complexities regarding the Divine—an exercise that could be as frustrating as a novice seeking to master a Rubik Cube. No, the divine mystery is clearly identified as "Christ in you, the hope of glory."

Paul continues, expressing the hope that his readers attain . . .

> . . . all the wealth that comes from the full assurance of understanding, resulting in a true knowledge of God's mystery, that is, Christ Himself, in whom are hidden all the treasures of wisdom and knowledge. (Colossians 2:2–3)

This passage contains exciting promises for the seeker of God.

1. A spiritual wealth will be attained.

2. There will be a complete assurance that one has been able to understand God.

3. The knowledge gained about God will be that which is true.

4. The mystery of God is revealed to be Christ.

5. In Christ is found real wisdom and knowledge.

These are all concepts that will communicate meaningfully to the folk Muslim. Another passage with potential as a bridge is 1 Corinthians 2:6–8,10:

> Yet we do speak wisdom among those who are mature; a wisdom, however, not of this age, nor of the rulers of this age, who are passing away; but we speak God's wisdom . . . which God predestined before the ages to our glory; the wisdom which none of the rulers of this age has understood; for if they had understood it, they would not have crucified the Lord of glory. . . . For to us God revealed them through the Spirit: for the Spirit searches all things, even the depths of God.

God's wisdom is here defined as a mystery. The rulers did not understand the wealth of the mystery. They were blinded to God's plan. But now, in this age, the Holy Spirit reveals all the deep secrets of God to those who come to Him through faith in Jesus Christ.

Another relevant passage is Ephesians 3:8–11:

> To me, the very least of all saints, this grace was given, to preach to the Gentiles the unfathomable riches of Christ, and to bring to light what is the administration of the mystery which for ages has been hidden in God, who created all things; in order that the manifold wisdom of God might now be made known through the church to the rulers and the authorities in the heavenly places. This was in accordance with the eternal purpose which He carried out in Christ Jesus our Lord.

Here we see the necessity of proclaiming the unlocked mystery of God. The "unfathomable riches of Christ" must be shared with all of God's creation. Muslim mystics will be drawn by the concept of mystery, but then, like Paul, they must see their responsibility to be "stewards of the mysteries of God" (1 Corinthians 4:1). Acceptance must lead to proclamation.

THE SUPERNATURAL

Consider the supernatural elements of this true story of three MBBs who were about to be killed because of their faith in Christ.

> The sun had reached its zenith hours ago and the afternoon was sultry and foreboding. The mob had conveniently arranged for men to come with bamboo poles, used to crack the skulls of wild animals or thieves. The three prayed, yet the first blow never came. Suddenly, a crazy man, who was known to be a spirit worshiper, burst into the ring of beaters. He was always a little weird, carrying chains and uttering incantations. At this moment he went from man to man staring at each and muttering in a monotone, "These men are righteous men; do not harm them; these men are righteous men; do not harm them." The village Muslim is an unorthodox breed, and the incantations of this man had a lot of weight. The religious leaders reconvened and decided that it was better not to beat them, but to have them all pray and show respect to Allah. The believers were delighted and prayed concluding each prayer in Jesus' name. After the trial was over, the crowd of Muslims dispersed. The crazy man was not to be found. One of the [MBBs] offered his explanation, "The crazy man was an angel."[16]

The effect of this supernatural intervention was worth more than a year's Bible-school training to these new MBBs. They were totally convinced God is alive and on their side. Is it not legitimate to expect God to do special things for His children in times of need? What about a sign from the Lord to a non-Christian in order to confirm His Word? I have known of several Muslims who have felt that God spoke to them through dreams. R. Max Kershaw comments,

> Two nights ago, a Muslim friend who was visiting in my home asked me what I thought about dreams. I told him

that the Bible contained many stories of dreams and their significance. He's been dreaming a lot of late and he's thinking about them. I have known several Muslim converts where dreams have been used as stepping stones to Christ.[17]

A missionary took an opportunity to witness to a Muslim for three hours one evening. It was evident the Lord was speaking to this young man, but his final response was, "I believe in what you say, but I want to wait for two months before I make a final decision to trust in Christ." Later that night the Muslim tossed and turned restlessly on his bed. In the early morning he finally drifted off to sleep.

The next day the missionary was surprised to receive a visit from the Muslim, who declared he was ready and eager to accept Christ immediately. When pressed for the reason for his change of mind, he told this story.

> After you left last night, I laid awake for several hours contemplating your words. When I finally got to sleep I had a dream about making the *Haj* to Mecca. In my dream I was so excited about being able to fulfill the deepest desire of my heart. I was traveling along a path with many curves. After each turn I eagerly looked ahead to see the skyline of the holy city of Mecca. My heart pounded with excitement. Each mile took me closer to God Himself. Then, at last, I realized that around the next curve I was to arrive in Mecca. Just as I came around the turn I saw—not Mecca, but a huge sign which said, "Follow the Holy Bible." I then awoke with the realization that I am to accept Christ as my Savior, I am ready now to believe.

Such is a documented testimony of the power of God being manifested through a dream. This young man is today a strong believer.

Another opportunity for witness involves healing. Illness is a serious problem among the poor. I have been deeply touched as I sit by the roadside in a Muslim village and watch masses of humanity pass by. At least one in five persons has an evident physical infirmity. For many, the cost of medicine is beyond their means. They will suffer curable illness for many years because of economic privation. The alternative, to many Muslims, is to seek help through the prayers of the *pirs*. Or many will perform a ritual, as I did. I went to a bearded Muslim sitting by the roadside and told him I wanted to purchase an amulet. He had a selection of Quranic verses printed on very thin paper laid out in front of him. He picked out one and explained the Arabic prayers that were written on it. After some typical haggling, I agreed to pay the demanded price, which was thirteen cents. The Muslim then began to quote Quranic verses while he stuffed the paper into a small metal casing which he then sealed with wax. He gave a beautiful prayer for my health and told me to always wear the amulet close to my body. He, being a good salesman, assured me he had other special amulets for children if I would be interested.

I asked another Muslim friend if he feels that amulets are effective in curing infirmities. He said they are for those who believe and they aren't for those who don't believe. This is not a bad answer. But isn't there a better way? Did not Christ consistently heal the sick? There is no recorded instance where Jesus refused to heal an individual. We are told in James 5:14 to pray over the sick and anoint them with oil in the name of the Lord. Many mystics could be persuaded to accept the gospel if they experienced healing as a result of a Christian's prayer.

ADAPTATIONS

Unfortunately, it is the foreign missionary who is usually in the vanguard of Muslim evangelism. He is either directly involved in or is indirectly supervising outreach. One can hope and pray for the day when a true indigenous church in each Muslim land is carrying out its own viable evangelistic program. Until that occurs, we must realistically analyze what we as foreign missionaries are exporting from our home culture in the West. All too often our ethnocentricity causes us to reproduce our total Western church program in our target country. Steeples, crosses, benches, pulpits, choirs, and organs create a huge psychological block to Muslims who have worshiped God all their lives with none of these things. I seriously question the wisdom of this methodology for witness in an Islamic country, James L. Barton, an unheeded prophet, wrote these insightful words in 1918:

> The Christian missionary in approaching the Mohammedan, must be ready to make concessions respecting Christian customs and traditions. This in no way implies that there must be a concession in Christian truth, but a concession in practices and methods. We have been altogether too fixed in our forms of preaching and of conducting church worship, when approaching the Mohammedan of the East. He is also fixed in his methods and is often repelled at the outset by what he sees and hears, when the things that repel him have no particular significance to Christian worship, doctrine, or life.[18]

In the next section of this chapter I will present the attempts of one group to contextualize a witness for Christ in a Muslim setting. It is much too early to be dogmatic about this type of approach. Time will allow us to make an accurate evaluation. However, a small group of observers has felt such adaptations to be syncretistic. I have sought to deal in depth with these issues in *Muslim Evangelism*. But I cannot resist quoting again from the evangelical Baptist Barton. Was he prophetic in the year 1918?

> It would be well for those who wish to get near to the Mohammedan and to remove prejudice and win his confidence, seriously to consider whether the buildings which stand for Christianity cannot wisely, and should not, for psychological purposes alone, be shorn of their ornamentation which is repulsive to those whom they wish to win. This is a matter for careful consideration in the construction of churches and all places of worship in countries where the Mohammedan is the special object of approach. Is there any reasonable objection, as many workers among Mohammedans have already suggested, to using the Muslim method of calling to Christian services? The minaret is a graceful addition to the place of worship. What could be more impressive than to have the call go out from the minaret in the name of the God

of heaven and the Savior of men, to all within the sound of the voice, summoning to the worship of God through Jesus Christ?[19]

Earlier in this chapter, I used a series of contrasts to highlight the problem of the Muslim's perception of the missionary (refer to table 1). Is it not right to prayerfully consider the whole question of image from the view of the receptor community? Perhaps missionaries should consider specific changes that would be appreciated by Muslims but would not involve any form of theological compromise.

For example, is *dhikr* an acceptable form for communicating Christ to mystics? "Professor D. B. Macdonald urges that *dhikr* be studied by the Christian missionaries with a view to discovering, if possible, some underlying principle or truth to aid in propagating Christianity among Muslims and especially among the followers of Sufism."[20] Can meditation on the names of God be a bridge that will move us close to the folk Muslim? I well remember the excruciating experience of hearing new MBBs try to sing hymns with Western tunes. Fortunately, the leader soon switched to Muslim tunes with Christian words. This was followed by enthusiastic chanting of "God is One" and "Jesus is Savior." Those converts were enjoying a meaningful worship experience that was dynamic but not overly emotional. It was in forms that were familiar and appreciated. Chanting is allowable in the mosques whereas singing is not. However, religious singing is very common among mystics outside the mosque. One Muslim writer has said, "Those who prohibit music do so in order that they may keep the Divine commandment, but theologians are agreed that it is permissible to hear musical instruments if they are not used for diversion, and if the mind is not led to wickedness through hearing them."[21] Music should be contextualized. Attempts should be made to have converts write original lyrics and set them to existing religious tunes or chants.

One last word needs to be said in regard to adaptation. The early Sufi missionaries to the Indian subcontinent were extremely successful. It is important to note that these men endured great sacrifice and privation. They possessed indomitable zeal for their task. How they longed to see the polytheistic Hindu turn from his idolatry to serve one God. Millions did. It is said that Sufis impressed the heathen with their saintlike qualities. They looked, acted, and preached like men sent from heaven. Love was the consuming motivation for their mission.

Now foreign missionaries are moving in to labor and preach among folk Muslims. The heart-searching question before us is: How will we be evaluated?

ALIPUR: A CASE STUDY

Relevant details of this case study are true, although certain descriptions and names have been altered in order to assure necessary anonymity. Alipur, a town with a population of sixty thousand, has a very small animist-background Christian community that is quite cut off from social interaction with the Muslim majority. Generally Muslims are friendly and religiously quite tolerant. Most of the people throughout the district are influenced by folk Islam.

In the early 1980s, the World Outreach Mission placed three foreign couples in Alipur. This summary of their ministry is based on these few brief months. The work is untested by time and is not presented as a model for success. Rather, it is given as a description of a cross-cultural ministry among Muslims in a pioneer setting. At the start of their ministry, there were no believers from a Muslim background and no Christian outreach was being attempted.

The three couples decided to work in five small towns in the district, I will focus on one missionary, Dan, and his evangelistic efforts in two of the towns, which will be designated A and B.

The missionaries made a study of local culture and then made these adaptations.

Dress that is common among Muslim religious leaders is worn by the missionary men. This is in contrast to Western clothes, which are worn by the majority of national men. The missionaries also have beards, which are a sign of a truly religious person. The wives wear clothes that are culturally acceptable to local people.

Dramas and movies are greatly enjoyed by the general populace, but religious leaders would never attend. Therefore, the missionary refrains from attending entertainment that by Western standards would be regarded as quite innocuous. Eating pork is believed by Muslims to be a major sin, so it is therefore avoided.

It is impossible for missionaries to live on the economic level of the religious leaders of Alipur. However, the foreigners have sought to live on as simple a level as physically and emotionally possible.

Muslims place great emphasis on that which is observable. Religion is to be expressed in terms of externals. Even mystics, who stress subjective experience, have their own systems of ritual that make them identifiable to others. In light of these facts, missionaries have sought to project an identity and to preach Christianity in terms that communicate effectively to their target audience.

Dan is privileged to work with an outstanding MBB who possesses unusual spiritual and intellectual qualities. Abdul is a volunteer worker who, with his wife, has agreed to labor for Christ in return for various gifts which are at best a subsistence allowance. Abdul, without doubt, would be a successful businessman if he left the ministry. The outreach in nearby villages A and B is very much a team effort. Muslims have been quick to acknowledge the spiritual gifts of Abdul and have categorized him as a special teacher rather than just an employee who is paid to preach the gospel.

The villages each had a population of fewer than a thousand. A small "office" was rented in each place. No signboards define the function of the rooms. The offices have no fans or furniture. Mats are laid out on the floor. Literature is placed on *riyals*, wooden stands on which holy books are placed). Arabic quotes extolling God have been colorfully painted on posters and hung on the walls.

Each of the villages is visited once a week, usually for a period of ten hours. The visits are made on a very regular basis so a pattern of familiarity is established. Dan and Abdul seek to make these visits together, but often, because of various circumstances, only one of them makes the trip.

The literature used in the offices is a series of specially prepared courses that are very carefully written in cultural and linguistic forms appreciated by Muslims. Covers of the books are decorated with eye-catching Islamic art forms. Each book has pages of questions to fill out and turn in. These courses are geared to personal contact. Doing the courses by mail is not encouraged.

Dan and Abdul do not distribute literature outside their offices. However, they do discreetly walk around and make contacts in the bazaars and the various shops. They avoid any type of profound religious discussions outside their office. Other foreigners are not encouraged to visit these villages. No pictures are taken of inquirers or new believers.

There have been some sensitive linguistic adjustments to the local situation. Muslims regard "Christians" as polytheistic worshipers of three gods, pork eaters, and wine drinkers. In an attempt to move the focus of attention from cultural Christianity to spiritual Christianity, the words *followers of Isa* are used. Arabic words that communicate meaningfully to Muslims are frequently used in conversation.

Prayer is offered with uplifted hands, as is the custom among Muslims. Chanting, as well as Islamic tunes, is used in worship. Spiritual dynamics are constantly emphasized.

There is no option for flight for new believers. They are told from the beginning that they must remain totally within their society. They are to carefully share their faith with relatives and friends. They are to *demonstrate* their faith before articulating it.

The aim of this work is to see a homogeneous, Muslim-background, worshiping group established in each village. Until the believers can afford to erect a building, meetings take place in homes. No financial assistance has been given to believers.

At a certain point, sufficient inquirers and MBBs were identified and a monthly meeting for Bible teaching and fellowship was commenced in Alipur. The men travel in from the villages at their own expense. Until now, the missionaries have paid for the simple meal that is served. However, some donations have been made by the believers to help offset the cost of the food. The men have been spiritually strengthened and stimulated by meeting others like themselves.

In the first year there have been nine clear professions of faith in villages A and B. All of these are from middle-aged men who are respected within their Muslim society. Several others are inquiring. Almost all of these are mystical in background. The significance of this small group lies in its contrast to the almost nonexistent Muslim-background Christian community in the country in which Alipur is located.

This case study is shared for the purpose of stimulating Christian workers to commence a ministry among Muslims where none presently exists. As Dan and Abdul would testify, such work requires a great deal of patience and tenacity—but the results make it eminently worthwhile.

(Afterword: By 2006, the number of MBBs in this general area of Alipur has grown to over 800.)

NOTES

1. Paul Hiebert, "Social Structure and Church Growth," in *Crucial Dimensions in World Evangelism*, ed. Arthur F. Glasser et al. (Pasadena, Calif.: William Carey Library, 1976), 63.

2. Charles R. Marsh, *Streams in the Sahara* (Bath, England: Echoes of Service, 1972), 32.

3. Bill Musk, "Popular Islam: The Hunger of the Heart," in *The Gospel and Islam: A 1978 Compendium*, ed. Don M. McCurry (Monrovia, Calif.: MARC, 1979), 215. Used by permission.

4. Arthur F. Glasser, "Power Encounter in Conversion from Islam," in *The Gospel and Islam: A 1978 Compendium*, ed. Don M. McCurry (Monrovia, Calif.: MARC, 1979), 137.

5. H. A. R. Gibb, *Mohammedanism: An Historical Survey* (New York: Oxford University, 1962), 133–134.

6. John A. Subhan, *Sufism: Its Saints and Shrines* (Lucknow: Lucknow Publishing House, 1938), 322.

7. Reynold A. Nicholson, *The Idea of Personality in Sufism* (1923; reprinted Delhi: Idarah-i Adabiyat-i Delli, 1976), 71.

8. Phil Parshall, *Muslim Evangelism* (Authentic: Tyrone, GA, 2003).

9. This list, originally given by Muhammad Al-Bakhari, is from Thomas P. Hughes, *Notes on Muhammadanism*, 3d ed. (London: W. H. Allen and Company, 1894), 249–253.

10. Subhan, *Sufism: Its Saints and Shrines*, 16.

11. Charles R. Marsh, *Too Hard for God* (Bath, England: Echoes of Service, 1970), 44–45.

12. Titus Burckhardt, *An Introduction to Sufi Doctrine*, trans. D. M. Matheson (Lahore: Shaikh Muhammad Ashraf, 1959), 8.

13. Nicholson, *Idea of Personality in Sufism*, 67.

14. David W. Shenk, "The [Sufi] Mystical Orders in Popular Islam" (unpublished paper, 1981), 11.

15. William Barclay, *The Letters to the Philippians, Colossians and Thessalonians* (Edinburgh: Saint Andrew Press, 1959), 120.

16. Parshall, *Muslim Evangelism*.

17. R. Max Kershaw, personal letter to the author, January 8, 1979, 1.

18. James L. Barton, *The Christian Approach to Islam* (Boston: Pilgrim Press, 1918), 257.

19. Ibid., 262.

20. Ibid., 203.

21. Ikbal Ali, *Islamic Sufism* (Delhi: Idarah-i Adabiyat-i Delli, 1933), 265–266.

A FINAL WORD

In recent years and in light of 9–11, Islam has become a subject of frequent analysis in the Western press. Secularists are seeking to understand a religious force of ancient vintage in light of twenty-first-century social and political norms. Because of differing perspectives and presuppositions, the analysis is little more than a caricature of the real situation. Muslims are castigated for maintaining a seventh-century mind-set. The West seeks to cajole and coax Islam into modernity. Muslims, for their part, evaluate so-called progress as the door to secularism and materialism. To many, this is religiously unacceptable and undesirable.

This is not to say that all Muslims are living in the past. Islamic nations have learned to use the political clout of oil in the same way the West has used the dollar in times past. Iran and Iraq have been willing to go to war to expand geographical boundaries.

Islam, then, is dynamic. It is multifaceted and complex. There are secular Muslims in leadership posts in fundamentalist Islamic nations. There are contradictions as well as consistencies.

Yet there are many similarities among individual Muslims. They desire to know God and to be accepted by Him. They have a high view of one God who is uniformly regarded as all-powerful and merciful. Mystics go on to press for a satisfying personal relationship with Allah. They may follow unorthodox paths to gain this experience, but most of them are sincere in the quest.

Do evangelical Christians really care about Muslims? Perhaps less than 5 percent of our missionary staff is assigned to Muslim countries. Approximately one-fifth of the world's population is Islamic. Certainly our response to the Muslim challenge has been grossly inadequate.

I dream of the day when Christians really begin to be concerned for the Muslim masses. When will we send our best young people to go forth in Christ's name to the hard places? Can we trust God to speak to mission societies and bring them to a place where they will reexamine well-established methodologies—if this is the will of God? What about finances? May we cry out to God for a flow of money to back up the frontline soldiers on the battlefield.

Some years back, a large Muslim country was in the throes of a bloody civil war. At about midpoint in the conflict I made a trip into a very remote area of this country for the purpose of distributing relief funds to starving people. Our little boat slowly made its way through the narrow canals. We carefully avoided the larger market towns, which were being bombed every few days.

At one point, my boatman asked me if I would like to visit a covert hospital that had been established to treat wounded freedom fighters. This involved a certain degree of risk, yet I was anxious to make contact with the brave young men who were fighting for the independence of their country.

Just at dusk we beached our boat and walked into an abandoned courtyard. There were five bamboo thatched huts around the edge of the clearance. A young man cordially greeted us and invited us into one of the small houses. Once inside, I was shocked to see a very handsome young man lying on a table and grimacing in pain as a nurse put a dressing on the stump of his amputated leg. He had been shot in a campaign against the opposing soldiers. It was a miracle he survived the ordeal.

Some minutes later, the boy hobbled out into the courtyard on crutches and began to chat with me. He had left the university to pursue a cause. He now was a cripple for life. I asked this very gracious patriot if he regretted his decision to join the guerillas. Never will I forget his answer. Without hesitation, he, with a faint smile playing on his lips, said, "No, no, never. If I had it to do all over again, I would gladly do it in order that my country be free!"

What a price to pay for political freedom. We as Christians are engaged in a battle for the spiritual liberation of souls. Are we willing to count the cost, move out into the front lines, suffer the reverses, endure the pains in the cause of presenting Christ to the Muslim world? Nothing less will enable us to experience the joys of victory—victories that become meaningful only after we have been in the fierce conflict where eternal destinies are determined.

The author invites correspondence at the following address:

Dr. Phil Parshall
PO Box 7900
Charlotte, NC 28241

GLOSSARY

Al-Junaid fana—the act of dying to self

Awliya—saint

Baqr Eid—Muslim festival that celebrates Abraham's willingness to sacrifice his son to God

Barakah—spiritual influence or blessing

Bismillah Rahmaner Rahim—"in the name of God, the beneficent, and merciful"

Chaitya-puja—Buddhist ceremony of worship at the graves of holy men

Chishti—one of the four major orders of Sufism

Darwish—wandering religious mendicant

Dhikr—ceremony that centers around the recitation of the names and attributes of God

Fana—total absorption into God

Faqir—religious person who solicits alms in the name of Islam

Folk Islam—Islam as it is practiced by adherents on grassroots level of society

Ganja—strong, mind-altering drug

Guru—Hindu spiritual leader

Hadith—Islamic traditions

Hagiology—book of saints' lives and legends

Haqiqah—"truth"; sixth stage of Sufism

Hooka—water pipe used for smoking tobacco or *ganja*

Imam—Islamic priest

Inshallah—"God willing"

Isai—"follower of Jesus"

Ishq—"love of God"; second stage of Sufism

Istikhara—a special mystical ceremony in which a Sufi makes a prayer request and expects the answer to come during a dream

Madrasa—Muslim religious school

Mantra—a word that has spiritual significance for an individual mystic

Marifah—"knowledge"; fourth stage of Sufism

Mazar—shrine of a departed Muslim mystic

Murid—follower of a *pir*

Murshid—spiritual guide

Nafs—the flesh

Naqshbandi—one of the four major orders of Sufism

Pir—mystically-oriented Muslim spiritual guide

Puja—Hindu worship ceremony

Qadiri—one of the four major orders of Sufism

Rikor—the last three days of the Muslim fast as observed in the Philippines

Riyal—wooden stand on which holy books are placed

Shariat—code of Islamic law

Sufism—mystically-oriented school of thought within Islam

Suhrawardi—one of the four major orders of Sufism

Sunnah—record of sayings and activities of Muhammad

Sura—chapter of the Quran

Tabbarukat—communication from a *pir* to his devotees who send him money or gifts

Tahil—recitation of "there is no God but God"

Tarika—a path or order within Sufism

Tawajjuh—power of concentration; method by which the *pir* transmits his spiritual power to his disciple

Therea—Buddhist word for "old man"; Buddhist counterpart of a *pir*

Tilawat—recitation of the Quran

Ubudiyah—"service"; first stage of Sufism

Urs—"marriage"; a union between the *pir* and God at the time of his death. This event is celebrated by disciples each year on the anniversary of the *pir's* death. The word also denotes the annual religious meeting of a living *pir.*

Wajd—"ecstasy"; fifth stage of Sufism

Wasl—"union with God"; seventh stage of Sufism

Zuhd—"seclusion"; third stage of Sufism

BIBLIOGRAPHY

Abbott, Freeland. *Islam and Pakistan.* Ithaca, N.Y.: Cornell University, 1968.

Abdul-Haqq, Abdiyah Akbar. *Sharing Your Faith with a Muslim.* Minneapolis: Bethany Fellowship, 1980.

Ahmad, Aziz. *Studies in Islamic Culture in the Indian Environment.* Oxford: Clarendon, 1964.

Ahmad, Hazrat Mirza Ghulam. *The Teachings of Islam.* Rabwah, Pakistan: Al-Tabshir (Ahmadiyya Muslim Foreign Missions), 1910.

Ahmad, Khurshid, ed. *Islam: Its Meaning and Message.* London: Islamic Council of Europe, 1976.

Ahmed, Sufia. *Muslim Community in Bengal, 1884–1912.* Dacca: Oxford University, 1974.

Ali, Anwar. *Islam: Ideology and Leading Issues.* Lahore: Publishers United, 1978.

Ali, Ikbal. *Islamic Sufism.* Delhi: Idarah-i Adabiyat-i Delli, 1933.

Ali, Syed Ameer, *The Spirit of Islam.* 1922. Reprint. London: Methuen, University Paperbacks, 1967.

Arasteh, A. Reza. *Rumi the Persian, the Sufi.* London: Routledge and Kegan Paul, 1974.

Arberry, A. J. "Mysticism." In *The Cambridge History of Islam.* Vol. 2. Edited by P. M. Holt, Anne K. S. Lambton, and Bernard Lewis. Cambridge: At the University Press, 1970.

———. *Sufism: An Account of the Mystics of Islam.* London: George Allen and Unwin, 1950.

Arnold, Sir Thomas, and Alfred Guillaume, eds. *The Legacy of Islam.* London: Oxford University, 1949 edition.

Atlas, Syed Naguib al. *Some Aspects of Sufism as Understood and Practised Among the Malays.* Singapore: Malaya Publishing House, 1963.

Azraf, Dewan Muhammad. *The Back-Ground of the Culture of Muslim Bengal.* Dacca: Islamic Foundation, 1971.

Azzam, Abd-al-Rahaman. *The Eternal Message of Muhammad.* Translated by Caesar E. Farah. New York: New American Library, 1964.

Barclay, William. *The Letters to the Philippians, Colossians and Thessalonians.* Edinburgh: Saint Andrew Press, 1959.

Barton, James L. *The Christian Approach to Islam.* Boston: Pilgrim Press, 1918.

Bethmann, Erich W. *Steps Toward Understanding Islam.* Kohinur series, no. 4. Washington, D.C.: American Friends of the Middle East, 1966.

Bhargava, K. D. *A Survey of Islamic Culture and Institutions.* Allahabad: Kitab Mahal, 1961.

Bhattacharyya, Haridas, ed. *The Cultural Heritage of India.* Vol. 4, *The Religions.* Calcutta: Ramakrishna Mission Institute of Culture, 1956.

Browne, Edward G. *A Literary History of Persia.* Vol. 1, *From the Earliest Times until Firdawsi.* New York: Cambridge University, 1951.

Bruno, Juanito A. *The Social World of the Tausug.* Manila: Centro Escolar University Research and Development Center, 1973.

Bulatao, Jaime. "The New Mysticism in the Philippine Church." Manila *Bulletin Today,* June 23, 1981, p. 6.

Burckhardt, Titus. *An Introduction to Sufi Doctrine.* Translated by D. M. Matheson. Lahore: Shaikh Muhammad Ashraf, 1959.

Calverley, Edwin Elliot. *Worship in Islam, being a translation with commentary and introduction of Al-Ghazzali's Book of the Ihya on the Worship.* Madras: Christian Literature Society for India, 1925.

Chapra, Hira Lal. "Sufism." In *The Cultural Heritage of India.* Edited by Haridas Bhattacharyya. Vol. 4, *The Religions.* Calcutta: Ramakrishna Mission Institute of Culture, 1956, pp. 593–610.

Cragg, Kenneth. *The Call of the Minaret.* New York: Oxford University, 1956.

————. *Sandals at the Mosque*. London: SCM, 1959.

Fatemi, Nasrollah S. *Sufism: Message of Brotherhood, Harmony, and Hope*. New York: A. S. Barnes, 1976.

Fatemi, S. Q. *Islam Comes to Malaysia*. Edited by Shirli Gordon. Singapore: Malaya Publishing House, 1963.

Fernea, Robert A., and Elizabeth W. Fernea. "Variation in Religious Observance among Islamic Women," In *Scholars, Saints and Sufis: Muslim Religious Institutions Since 1500*. Edited by Nikkie R. Keddie. Los Angeles: University of California, 1972, pp. 385–401.

Fry, C. George, and James R. King. *Islam: A Survey of the Muslim Faith*. Rev. ed. Grand Rapids: Baker, 1982.

Gibb, H. A. R. *Mohammedanism: An Historical Survey*. New York: Oxford University, 1962.

Gibb, H. A. R., and J. H. Kramers. *Shorter Encyclopedia of Islam*. Leiden: Brill, 1953.

Glasser, Arthur F. "Power Encounter in Conversion from Islam." In *The Gospel and Islam: A 1978 Compendium* Edited by Don M. McCurry. Monrovia, Calif.: MARC, 1979, pp. 129–139.

Gowing, Peter G. *Muslim Filipinos—Heritage and Horizon*. Quezon City: New Day Publishers, 1979.

Gowing, Peter G., and Robert D. McAmis. *The Muslim Filipinos*. Manila: Solidaridad Publishing House, 1974.

Gowing, Peter G., and William Henry Scott, eds. *Acculturation in the Philippines*. Quezon City: New Day Publishers, 1971.

Haq, Mahfuz-ul. *Socio-Religious Tradition of Islam*. Faridpur, Bangladesh: Rashidul Hassan, 1980.

Haq, Muhammad Enamul. *A History of Sufi-ism in Bengal*. Dacca: Asiatic Society of Bangladesh, 1975.

Haque, Tamizul. "Islam and Sufism." Unpublished paper, Dacca, March 5, 1982.

Hasan, S. M. *Muslim Creed and Culture*. Dacca: Ideal Publications, 1962.

Hiebert, Paul. "Social Structure and Church Growth." In *Crucial Dimensions in World Evangelization*. Edited by Arthur F. Glasser et al. Pasadena, Calif: William Carey Library, 1976, pp. 61–74.

Holt, P. M., Anne K. S. Lambton, and Bernard Lewis, eds. *The Cambridge History of Islam*. Vol. 1, *The Central Islamic Lands*. Cambridge: At the University Press, 1970.

————. *The Cambridge History of Islam.* Vol. 2, *The Further Islamic Lands, Islamic Society and Civilization.* Cambridge: At the University Press, 1970.

Hughes, Thomas P. *A Dictionary of Islam.* London: W. H. Allen, 1895.

————. *Notes on Muhammadanism.* 3d ed. London: W. H. Allen, 1894.

Husain, Sahibzada Syed Riyasat. "Urs Mubarak 1981 of Hazrat Khwaja Moinuddin Chishty (R. A.) Ajmir Sharif [India]." Handbill advertising a meeting, 1981.

Husaini, Moulavi S. A. Q. *Ibn Al 'Arabi, The Great Muslim Mystic and Thinker.* Lahore: Shaikh Muhammad Ashraf, 1931.

Isidro, Antonio, and Mamitua Saber. *Muslim Philippines.* Marawi City: University Research Center, Mindanao State University, 1968.

"Islamic Mysticism," *Encyclopaedia Britannica, Macropaedia,* 1974 edition, vol. 9, pp. 943–948.

Jafar, Abu. *Muslim Festivals in Bangladesh.* Dacca: Islamic Foundation, 1980.

Jones, L. Bevan. *The People of the Mosque.* Calcutta: YMCA Publishing House, 1939.

Jones, Violet Rhoda, and L. Bevan Jones. *Woman in Islam.* Lucknow: Lucknow Publishing House, 1941.

Karim, Anwarul. *The Bauls of Bangladesh.* Kushtia: Lalon Academy, 1980.

Kershaw, R. Max Personal letter to the author, January 8, 1979.

Khan, Hazrat Inayat. *The Sufi Message of Hazrat Inayat Khan.* Vols. 2,7, 9,12. London: Barrie and Rockliff, 1960, 1962, 1963, 1967.

Klein, F. A. *The Religion of Islam.* London: Kegan Paul, Trench, Trubner, 1906.

Krishna, Lajwanti Rama. *Panjabi Sufi Poets A.D. 1460–1900.* Karachi: Indus Publishers, 1977.

McAmis, Robert D. "Characteristics of Southeast Asian Islam as Factors in a Theology of the Christian Mission to Philippine Muslims." Unpublished dissertation, Concordia Seminary, Saint Louis, Mo. 1967.

Madale, Abdullah. *The Remarkable Maranaws.* Quezon City: Omar Publications, 1976.

Madale, Nagasura. "Ramadhan as Observed in Lanao." *Mindanao Journal,* vol. 1, no. 3, 1975, pp. 15–24.

Majul, Cesar Adib. *Muslims in the Philippines.* Quezon City: University of the Philippines, 1973.

Marsh, Charles R. *Streams in the Sahara.* Bath, England: Echoes of Service, 1972.

―――. *Too Hard for God.* Bath, England: Echoes of Service, 1970.

Maududi, Sayyid Abul A'la. *A Short History of the Revivalist Movement in Islam.* Translated by Al-Ash'ari. Lahore: Islamic Publications, 1972.

Milctitch, Nicolas. "Kremlin Is Worried Over Islamic Minorities." Manila *Bulletin Today.* July 19,1981.

Mujeeb, M. *The Indian Muslims.* London: George Allen and Unwin, 1967.

Musk, Bill. "Popular Islam: The Hunger of the Heart." In *The Gospel and Islam: A 1978 Compendium.* Edited by Don M. McCurry. Monrovia, Calif.: MARC, 1979, pp. 208–221.

―――. "Roles: God, Communicator, Muslim." Special project for Dean S. Gilliland, Fuller Theological Seminary, Pasadena, Calif., 1978.

Nasr, Seyyed Hossein. *Ideals and Realities of Islam.* London: George Allen and Unwin, 1966.

―――. *Living Sufism.* London: Unwin Paperbacks, 1972.

―――. "The Western World and Its Challenges to Islam." In *Islam: Its Meaning and Message.* Edited by Khurshid Ahmad. London: Islamic Council of Europe, 1976, pp. 217–41.

Nehls, Gerhard. *And What about the Muslim?* Bellville, South Africa: Evangelical Mission Press, 1980.

Nicholson, Reynold A. *The Idea of Personality in Sufism.* 1923. Reprint. Delhi: Idarah-i Adabiyat-i Delli, 1976.

―――. "Mysticism." In *The Legacy of Islam.* Edited by Sir Thomas Arnold and Alfred Guillaume. London: Oxford University, 1949 edition, pp. 210–238.

―――. *The Mystics of Islam.* London: Routledge and Kegan Paul, 1914.

―――. *Studies in Islamic Mysticism.* Cambridge: At the University Press, 1921.

Nuruddin, Abu Sayeed. *Allama Iqbal's Attitude Toward Sufism and His Unique Philosophy of Khudi-self.* Dacca: Islamic Foundation, 1978.

Padwick, Constance E. *Muslim Devotions: A Study of Prayer-Manuals in Common Use.* London: S.P.C.K, 1961.

Parshall, Phil. *The Fortress and the Fire.* Bombay: Gospel Literature Service, 1975.

————. *Muslim Evangelism.* Tyrone, GA: Authentic, 2003.

Pasha, Mustafa Halimi. *Tarikh-i-Tasawwuf-i-Islam.* Translated by Rayees Ahmad Jafri. Lahore: n.p., 1950.

Rahman, H. "Anomalies." In Reader's Forum of *The* [Dacca] *New Nation,* March 15, 1981, p. 5.

Rasul, Fiscal Jainal D. *The Philippine Muslims: Struggle for Identity.* Manila: Neuva Era Press, 1970.

Saber, Mamitua, and Abdullah T. Madale, eds., *The Maranao.* Manila: Solidaridad Publishing House, 1975.

Sarangani, Datumanong Di A. "Islamic Penetration in Mindanao and Sulu." *Mindanao Journal,* vol. 3, no. 3–4, January-June 1977, pp. 29–53.

Sattar, E. M. *Ibn Khaldun, the Author of the Muqaddimah.* Dacca: Islamic Foundation, 1980.

Schaeffer, Francis A. *The God Who Is There.* Downers Grove, Ill.: Inter-Varsity, 1968.

Seale, Morris S. *Muslim Theology.* London: Luzac and Company, 1964.

Shah, Idries. *Oriental Magic.* Tonbridge, England: Octagon Press, 1968.

————. *The Sufis.* Garden City, N.Y.: Doubleday, 1971.

————. *The Way of the Sufi.* New York: Dutton, 1970.

Sharif, M. M. *Muslim Thought: Its Origin and Achievements.* Lahore: Shaikh Muhammad Ashraf, 1951.

Shehadi, Fadlou. *Ghazali's Unique Unknowable God.* Leiden: Brill, 1964.

Shenk, David W. "The [Sufi] Mystical Orders in Popular Islam." Unpublished paper, 1981.

Shushtery, A. M. A. *Outlines of Islamic Culture.* Vol. 1, *Historical and Cultural Aspects.* Bangalore: Bangalore Press, 1938.

Sioson-San Juan, Thelma. "Mt. Banahaw: a world rooted in religion." Manila *Times Journal,* June 24, 1981, p. 4.

Smith, Wilfred Cantwell. *Islam in Modern History.* New York: New American Library, Mentor Books, 1957.

Subhan, John A. *Sufism: Its Saints and Shrines.* Lucknow: Lucknow Publishing House, 1938.

Sweetman, J. W. *The Bible in Islam.* London: British and Foreign Bible Society, n.d.

Trimingham, J. Spencer. *A History of Islam in West Africa.* London: Oxford University, 1962.

———. *The Influence of Islam upon Africa.* London: Longmans, Green, 1968.

———. *Islam in West Africa.* Oxford: Clarendon, 1959.

———. *The Sufi Orders in Islam.* Oxford: Clarendon, 1971.

Valiuddin, Mir. *Contemplative Disciplines in Sufism.* London: East-West Publications, 1980.

Venkatavaradan, V. S. "A Genius Called Abdus Salam." *The Illustrated Weekly of India,* February 1–7, 1981, pp. 25ff.

Von Grunebaum, G. E. "Islam, Essays in the Nature and Growth of a Cultural Tradition." *The American Anthropologist,* vol. 57, no. 2, pt. 2, memoir no. 81, April 1955.

———. "Studies in Islamic Cultural History." *The American Anthropologist,* vol. 56, no. 2, pt. 2, memoir no. 76, April 1954.

Watt, W. Montgomery. *The Faith and Practice of Al-Ghazali* London: George Allen and Unwin, 1953; Lahore: Shaikh Muhammad Ashraf, 1953.

Welch, Alford T., and Pierre Cachia, eds. *Islam: Past Influence and Present Challenge.* Edinburgh: University Press, 1979.

Wells, William. Personal letter to the author, May 20, 1981.

Wulff, Inger. "Continuity and Change in a Yakan Village." *Dansalan Quarterly,* vol. 1, no. 3, April 1980, pp. 149–168.

Zwemer, Samuel M. *Islam: A Challenge to Faith.* New York: Student Volunteer Movement for Foreign Missions, 1907.

SUBJECT INDEX

Scripture Index